LIFE
AFTER LUST

STORIES & STRATEGIES FOR SEX
& PORNOGRAPHY ADDICTION RECOVERY

BY
FOREST BENEDICT, LMFT, SATP

Advance Acclaim for "Life After Lust"

"Forest's book *Life After Lust* is a valuable contribution to the sex addiction treatment field."

> – **Mark Laaser, M.Div., Ph.D.**, Pioneer in the field of sex addiction recovery, Author of *The Fight of Your Life*, President & Founder of Faithful & True

"Forest Benedict offers a fresh resource for pornography addicts and those struggling with other forms of sexual addiction. His framework of *"mindset, mastery,* and *mission"* goes beyond the familiar principles of recovery to focus extensively on self-care in a way that's lacking in most resources. *Life After Lust* is an extremely practical and specific book that is rich with Benedict's humility and lessons learned in his personal recovery process. As a clinician who works extensively with female sex addicts, I especially appreciate that *Life After Lust* includes women among those who struggle. I highly recommend this book and am grateful to have it as a preferred resource."

> – **Marnie C. Ferree, LMFT, CSAT**, Author of *No Stones – Women Redeemed from Sexual Addiction* and Director of

Bethesda Workshops, a Christian-based intensive program for sex addicts and their partners. www.BethesdaWorkshops.org

"Life After Lust is an honest and helpful read for those trapped in the fear and pain of pornography addiction. This book challenges men and women to take responsibility for their behavior, providing practical tools and next steps on their healing journey."

> – **Craig Gross**, Founder of XXXchurch.com

"Forest Benedict's *Life After Lust* is a personalized and important contribution to the field of sexual health. He shares his personal story of recovery from porn addiction in a way that both educates and motivates the reader."

> – **Robert Weiss, LCSW, CSAT-S**, Intimacy Disorder
> Specialist, Author of *Out of the Doghouse: A Step-by-Step*
> *Relationship-Saving Guide for Men Caught Cheating*

"Life After Lust is a thorough and thoughtful guide to recovery from sex addiction. In it, Benedict provides a step-by-step roadmap for the journey from addiction to freedom."

> – **Douglas Weiss, Ph.D.**, Author of *Clean*, President of
> the American Assoc. for Sex Addiction Therapy

"Forest Benedict's book *Life After Lust* is a gift for those struggling with problematic sexual behavior, those who love them, and professionals who work with them. Forest provides the reader with a uniquely important perspective on this complex issue. His personal understanding as a fellow struggler, blended with his professional wisdom and experience, gives us a powerfully credible voice of warning, practical healing tools, and a passionate message of hope."

> – **Dan Gray, LCSW, CSAT**, Co-founder of the LifeStar Network

"Let's admit it, sexual addiction recovery is anything but simple and cannot be approached with a set of anecdotal answers. As a past SATP student of mine, I couldn't be more proud of Forest and this book. Forest brings his own humble journey of recovery, along with a robust and scientific understanding of what works to bring real change for those who struggle in this area. His heart for others and appetite for learning have moved him from student to expert. Now he passes this onto you. You will experience hope by taking this journey with him."

> – **Todd Frye, Ph.D., LCPC, LCMFT, SATP-S, NCC**, Dean of Behavioral Sciences and Counseling, Mid-America Nazarene University.

"Forest Benedict is a skilled writer whose lyrical phrases delight and uplift this intense topic. Addiction-savvy and trauma-informed, Benedict never lets up on his fierce, loving message: **Yes, you can do this! You will have to work hard to beat sex addiction, but I've done it, it's worth it, and I'm right here with you!** *Life After Lust* is a must-read for any man, woman or loving family member who needs unrelenting optimism and cutting-edge strategies that really work on the road to healthy sexuality."

> – **Staci Sprout, LICSW, CSAT**, author of *Naked in Public: A Memoir of Recovery From Sex Addiction and Other Temporary Insanities*

"*Life After Lust* is a ready reference guide for sex addicts in any stage of recovery and the therapists who work with them. Throughout his remarkable book, Forest provides a solid recovery path; a path that leads to connection with God, self, and others. I have treated sex addicts and their families for the past 29 years and I look forward to using this book with my clients. I will recommend *Life After Lust* to addicts, clergy, and therapists."

      – **Todd Olson, LCSW,** Co-Founder of the LifeSTAR
      Network

"Forest does a masterful job of touching on the root issues of sex addiction without getting too "heady." But he also does an equally masterful job of providing tons of time-tested, practical counsel to male and female strugglers who need real handles. Rarely do you find someone who can do both and respect the reader's belief in God at the same time. This is an invaluable resource for counselors, pastors, and strugglers alike."

      – **Russell Willingham**, Executive Director, Fresno New
      Creation Ministries, Author of *Breaking Free:*
      Understanding Sexual Addiction and *The Healing Power of*
      Jesus

"*Life After Lust* is a resource to help reinforce you for a lifetime of healthy living. While it's not easy to stop a pornography or sex addiction, it's even more difficult to build a life of trust, intimacy, connection, and emotional health after years of addictive living. Forest has taken a complicated and confusing process and organized it into an easy-to-follow guide. Knowing Forest, he would love to sit down with each person who picks up his book and personally help them map out their own journey.

Thankfully, anyone who reads this book will feel like they're sitting with him getting personal guidance and support. His compassionate and non-judgmental voice comes through loud and clear. He expects great things from his readers and offers encouragement and realistic goals to help people create a bright future."

> – **Geoff Steurer, MS, LMFT**, Founding Director of LifeStar of St. George, UT and co-author of *Love You, Hate the Porn: Healing a Relationship Damaged by Virtual Infidelity*

"Benedict offers a concrete, no-nonsense approach to overcoming sexually compulsive behaviors through looking in, looking out, and looking up for strength, support, and success in self-mastery, addiction recovery, and change. Anyone caught up in the snare of sexual addiction will benefit from using the tools within these pages."

> – **Debra W. Greeff, LCSW, SATP**, LifeStar Boise, Idaho

"Sex addiction destroyed my first marriage, so I was worried this book would be a trigger for me. But surprisingly, it was not! Benedict handles the topic in an incredibly powerful, insightful, yet sensitive manner. I am convinced that if more couples approached addiction recovery with these tools, there would be fewer divorces and less heartache. I applaud Benedict's courage in sharing his story and bestowing his hard-gained wisdom on others traveling this difficult path. I sincerely appreciate the emphasis on protecting children and standing against pornography. The chapter, *Dear Porn: A Father's Letter*, is close to my heart and truly a call to arms. As a mother and activist, I face this battle every day. Forest Benedict is a powerful ally in the fight!"

> – **Melody A. Bergman**, Writer, Speaker, Activist, Mamacrossroads.com

"I believe Forest's book, *Life After Lust*, is a valuable resource in the toolbox for every recovering sex addict. Forest's approach is refreshingly straightforward and laid out in strategies that are easy to follow for anyone seeking sobriety. The personable attention Forest gives from his own journey of recovery provides hope and encouragement to those who struggle with sexual addiction. This book will definitely be on my recommendation list for all my clients."

> – **Eli Machen, LCSW**, Pioneer in the field of sex addiction recovery, Author, Speaker, Therapist, @Showup365

"*Life After Lust* is an insightful read that validates the very real need for hard work, honesty, and personal responsibility in recovery. It is refreshing to find a book that is written openly and un-apologetically for men *and women* caught in the snares of pornography and sexual addiction. Forest's commentary is both timely and relevant."

> – **Lacy Alajna Bentley**, Founder of Women United Recovery Coalition, Recovering Relationship and Pornography Addict

"In his powerful book, *Life after Lust*, author and sex addiction therapist Forest Benedict explores the depths of lust, infidelity, and sex addiction, sharing practical, proven insights and a well-paved road to freedom. In the book, Forest vulnerably shares his own story of successful recovery, offering real hope for those wondering if life after lust is possible. I have worked with Forest in the SATP program, training counselors to help those trapped in sexual addiction. Forest is wise, compassionate, and incredibly insightful, providing a voice of experience, knowledge, and leadership in our field. You know someone in your life right now who desperately needs to read this book. I give my highest recommendation and praise for my friend and colleague Forest Benedict and his new book *Life After Lust*."

> – **Jim Cress, MA, LPC, CSAT**, Author, Speaker, Veteran Broadcaster, Founder and President of Integrity Redeemed Workshops. Charlotte, NC

"As an addict in recovery, a father, and a therapist, Forest shares experience and insights in his book that highlight key principles of healthy living. As such, *Life After Lust* is not just a book that benefits those struggling with sexual addiction. My invitation is for parents — and others concerned about the risks associated with raising children in a digital world — to read this book. Forest's honest storytelling and professional perspectives offer gems of wisdom that can help you be a better parent and person. I am grateful to Forest for his willingness to share his story to help others know not just how to heal from addiction, but also how to prevent it. Deliberate, connected, purposeful living is the key. Raising children in this way, I believe we have the chance to turn the tide on the plague of pornography impacting our young people today."

> – **Michelle Linford**, Executive Director, EPIK Deliberate Digital Kids

"*Life After Lust* is a comprehensive resource that provides fresh hope. Whether you're new to this journey or have been in recovery for years, this resource is for you. *Life After Lust* has practical tools to help sex addicts overcome lust, helping their loved ones understand the addictive experience as well. Forest does an amazing job passionately and vulnerably sharing his personal and professional experience. He is a warrior fighting the battle against lust with his words and actions. Join him in the journey today!"

> – **Cory Schortzman, MA, LPC, SRT,** Executive Director of Transformed Hearts Counseling Center, Founder of the Sex Addiction Recovery Association (SARA)

"I met Forest when I was active in my addiction. He came alongside me, loved me, and led me into recovery. Forest's heart for others is in this book. *Life After Lust* is a conduit for soul connection; a would-be syllabus for doctoral studies in personal recovery. With Forest's guidance, I am gratefully experiencing *life after lust*. I know this book will help others down this same path to healing."

> – **Anonymous Recovering Sex Addict, M. Div,** Former Pastor

"Forest Benedict, LMFT, SATP has written a powerful and timely must-read book for anyone struggling with pornography addiction. Read this book, learn from a professional who has 'been there' and let it change your life."

> – **Stacey B. Thacker, LMFT**, Roubicek and Thacker Counseling (LifeSTAR of the Central Valley), co-founder Lifestyle Transformation a treatment program for food addiction

"I have had the pleasure of knowing Forest for more than 10 years, but I have also enjoyed working with him in the field of sexual addiction. Before his career started, I saw him not only pursue recovery with great alacrity, but I also witnessed his transformation into someone with amazing integrity. He lived and breathed recovery to the point where he decided to become a therapist and help others out of the bondage of sexual addiction. The old adage, "There is no healer like a wounded healer" rings quite true with Forest. He has endeavored arduously to come out of the proverbial pit; he found the way out, and now, he wants to share his triumph with others. I am proud to work alongside this gifted writer and therapist, but more importantly, I am proud to call him my friend."

– Invia A. Betjoseph, PsyD, LMFT, CSAT

"A great satisfaction for a teacher is when the student not only excels in the acquisition of the material, but also exceeds in its application. Forest has done just that with his career, his writings, and now *Life After Lust*. The book is a skillful and compassionate use of his journey, offering the reader the opportunity to identify and then choose to use this information for their personal recovery. Forest organizes the material into the three M's of *Mindset*, *Mastery*, and *Mission*, punching the truths home. There is no way to avoid the destructive realities of sex addiction. But the reader is not left in misery. Hope comes through understanding the nature of the problem, which is then reinforced with action items for recovery. The final section of the book, called the *Recovery Roadmap*, is a masterful addition which supports the addict into long-term recovery—beyond successful sobriety—by practicing the tools of change. This section is also ideal for an aftercare group. Forest, you have given the recovering community a gift. On their behalf, I say *"Thank You."* Well done, you've made this teacher proud."

> – **Mary Anne Fifield, DMFT, CAS, CSAT**, Founding Director of the Addiction Recovery Center, San Jose, CA

"Forest's passion for helping those trapped in the chains of lust is epic. His willingness to be vulnerable and authentic as he shares his own story of recovery provides hope for those who believe there is no hope. The tools, insights, and guidelines provided in *Life After Lust* are a true gem."

> – **Troy Love, LCSW**, LifeSTAR of Yuma, AZ

"As a recovering female sex addict, I deeply appreciate the honesty and openness Forest models in his book *Life After Lust*. As female addicts, we spend most of our lives hiding in shame, thinking something is wrong with us. The truth is, we are just like Forest. *Life After Lust* is a great resource with real stories of real struggles, providing real hope."

> – **Anonymous Recovering Female Sex Addict**

"Coming alongside Forest in our mutual battle against pornography addiction has been both a blessing and an honor. Our recovery stories are very similar. We both started using pornography at a young age and have both found freedom from the lies, the shame, and the guilt. Forest's passion for helping others find freedom has led him to his career path as a sex addiction therapist and fueled his writing of *Life After Lust*. This book is amazing. In it, Forest presents a *Recovery Roadmap* that I truly believe will be a key factor in helping many men and women experience recovery. I cannot wait to hear the success stories of those who have not only read *Life After Lust* but applied the principles to their daily life, experiencing lasting freedom from the grips of pornography addiction."

> – **Stuart Tutt,** Recovering Pornography Addict, Blogger at *Something to Stu Over*, Founder of *Resurrecting the Redeemed from Porn Addiction*

"*Life After* Lust is an excellent resource for those wanting freedom from pornography addiction. This book also prepares men and women to fight for love in their personal relationships while working to change the world we live in."

> – **Clay Olsen,** CEO and Co-Founder of Fight the New Drug

LIFE AFTER LUST
Stories & Strategies for Sex & Pornography Addiction Recovery

Visionary Books, LLC
www.visionarybooks.org

ISBN: 0-9984682-1-5
ISBN-13: 978-0-9984682-1-1

Dedication

For my children, clients, and students — I believe in you!

Table of Contents

Foreword

As an addiction counselor of 20 years, I have attended many conferences and read many recovery-oriented books on sexual addiction. Forest Benedict's book, *Life After Lust,* provides a unique and important contribution to the field of sexual addiction recovery. For those who feel stuck in sexual addiction and desire a new life, you have the right book in your hands.

On a weekly basis, I hear clients share their relapse stories. Their accompanying feelings are often a mix of shame, hopelessness, and confusion about why and how this pernicious habit continues to rob them of their hope, dignity, and self-confidence. Without a solid recovery plan, life-damaging consequences continue to mount as week after week the addicts, in their own efforts, struggle in despair, searching for a pathway out of the chaos.

Life After Lust is written by a man who is not only a sexual addiction specialist, but who actively lives out his own recovery from sexual addiction. With 12 years of sobriety under his belt, Forest is able to share his story in an authentic manner that awakens hope in the reader. Each chapter provides both the road signs and building materials for a new path into a successful recovery. Personally, I have struggled with addictions in many areas of my life. When I read *Life After Lust* I was inspired, self-reflective, and motivated to be a better person. I hope you have the same experience.

Last year I invested a significant amount of time and money to complete the training to become certified as a sexual addiction therapist (CSAT). The professional organization that has trained nearly 1,500 CSATs is the International Institute of Trauma and Addiction Professionals. Many consider the founder, Dr. Patrick Carnes, to be the pioneer researcher and developer of sexual addiction recovery treatment. Since the four modules are fresh in my memory, I can attest that Forest's book is congruent with the most current research and the best practices of sexual addiction recovery.

The book is organized into three sections. The first section teaches you the *Essential Mindsets* necessary for a strong and successful recovery. It is common for many addicts to experience false hope with white-knuckle stretches of sobriety only to be deeply discouraged by chronic relapses. The mindsets offered here will equip you with the necessary focus for a strong and effective recovery plan.

The second section of the book presents specific *Skills to Master,* which are strategies for deepened recovery, achieved through the practice and mastery of recovery principles. Since addiction embeds itself deep within an individual, daily self-care practices, recovery rituals, and increased self-awareness are crucial for success. This section provides clear direction in these important areas.

The third section challenges you to pursue specific *Missions to Accomplish* as your recovery progresses. Here, Forest "calls you up" to identify ways you can personally make a difference in the world. This section echoes the message of The Twelfth Step of

Sexaholics Anonymous, which challenges recovering sex addicts to invest in others and to live out the principles as necessary by-products of their personal transformation. [1] Forest shares examples of ways he has chosen to take a stand and make a difference for good. He invites you to consider ways you can join the ranks to fight for your virtue as well as the virtue in your community and world.

As the founder of the LoneSTAR Coalition Against Pornography, which educates the public on the harmful effects of pornography, I appreciate how Forest connects recovery to protecting children from pornography, advocating against the pornography industry, and living in alignment with your deepest values. As you read the *Missions* section, I am confident that you will feel inspired to give back to others as a result of your own personal awakening through recovery.

Knowledge is power. Many addicts feel powerless over their addiction. Identifying and mastering recovery principles is the process that will help you to gain a sense of power in both your recovery and your personal life. *Life After Lust* features a wide variety of recovery principles that Forest has carefully chosen for the reader. Several of Forest's chapters in this book were previously published in his local newspaper, as a guest writer for XXX Church, for Protect Young Minds, and on his work and personal blogs. These articles were well received in the recovery community. In short, the recovery principles found in this book have been tried and tested. They have proven helpful to those in recovery. Even as I read the book, I felt within me an increased desire to improve personally, as well as a longing to reach out to the broader community, encouraging others to come out of the shadows and get help.

I have known Forest first as a respected colleague and now as a close friend. We see each other at the annual LifeSTAR conference and talk by phone regularly. This increased connection has allowed me the opportunity to get to know some of Forest's unique strengths and talents. Forest is a gifted writer. Here are just a few of my favorite quotes that demonstrate his ability to articulate complex ideas into meaningful phrases:

"So many are struggling, yet so few seek help. Shame is The Great Silencer."

"This section will challenge you to the core. You will be called out and called up."

"Love is the antidote to lust; healing happens through connection."

My wife and I can each name two to three significant people in our life who we describe as having the "heart of a teacher." Specifically, these teachers seem to have a deep sense of knowing and their life passion and gift is to teach and share this knowledge with others. I love to meet and learn from these gifted teachers. Forest definitely has the "heart of a teacher." The tone of his book is a pleasant mix of inspiration, education, and practical principles. I am confident that as you read the book, you will experience the heart of this teacher yourself.

As you begin this book, imagine yourself starting your first extreme mountaineering experience. You may feel overwhelmed at the task at hand as you gaze upward at the monumental climb ahead of you. Forest is your competent climbing guide. Since he personally has climbed this mountain and guided many others on the climb, be reassured that the hike will be safe and successful. It is important that you are proactive with the guidance given. For this to be a true experience of learning and growth, action is required, as is getting up after a fall.

As you listen to Forest's voice in the pages of this book, I am confident that you will feel inspired, guided, and strengthened. The rewards of recovery will be realized and your recovery vistas will be clearer as you reach many new summits of personal growth and awareness.

ENJOY the adventure and journey of recovery. It is well worth the climb!

- Shane Adamson, LCSW, EFT, CSAT-C, LifeSTAR Dallas, LoneSTAR Coalition Against Pornography

Introduction

“That's the last time. I'm done with this!” I can't count the times these words have rolled out of my mouth regarding my insatiable longing for lust. Sometimes that heartfelt commitment lasted days. Often it merely lingered for moments. Auto-pilot eventually kicked in and I would tumble back into the trance of temptation. Guided by an unseen force, I escaped into numbing and negligent behavior. Sometimes this meant drowning in a dozen dark hours, searching for the *perfect* porn. Often this meant drinking in sensual sights, using women to maintain my continual high. Many times this meant much worse. I would return to what was risky, search for what was secretive, and ride the rush into the shores of shame. Drenched in despair, unable to look anyone in the eyes, I would again utter the sincere yet empty phrase, “That's the last time. I'm done with this!”

And the cycle continued…for years.

Does this pattern of defeat describe your life experience? These days countless people feel first-hand the suffocating grip of sexual addiction. [2] There is no demographic for this destructive behavior. Women and men. Children and the elderly. Christians and atheists. Professionals and the impoverished.

None of us are protected from the pull of pornography or from the attraction to other avenues of acting out. This is a pandemic. Our world is saturated with sexual addiction.

So many are struggling, yet so few seek help. Shame is The Great Silencer. Feeling uniquely broken, they stand alone in the shadows.

When someone finally submits to the dreaded idea of finding help, it is often in the wake of devastating personal cost. They don't humbly reach for help until they are humbled by painful consequences. This is never a pretty sight. Their path to treatment is paved with trauma and tears. Why would they wait and pay such a price?

Fear.

Fear of being seen. Fear of admitting momentary defeat. Fear of feeling ashamed. Fear of trusting others. Ironically, fear of present pain keeps them postponing their healing. Yet this form of procrastination piles up unprecedented pain for the future. This thinking is a trap. We will all experience pain. Jim Rohn wisely wrote: "We must all suffer from one of two pains: the pain of discipline or the pain of regret. The difference is discipline weighs ounces while regret weighs tons."[3]

Do not let the pain of regret have the final word. I invite you to wake from your addictive stupor. Seize the opportunity before you. Use this manual to motivate you. Show your resilience and stand for what you know is right. Just like I challenge my clients, I challenge you: do not let yourself be immobilized by feelings of *shame*.[4] Instead, let the goodness of *guilt* mobilize you to proactive movement[5] (Chapter 17 discusses the difference between guilt and shame).

I have risen out of the shadows of sexual addiction. Now my life's work is helping others do the same. As a therapist who specializes in sexual addiction treatment, I have guided many who were willing to grow. I write, speak, and teach to this end: that those feeling trapped would find the courage to reach out and that those who have reached out would create the consistency that leads to lasting change.

This book is not meant for just men. While my stories are based on my male experience, it is my hope that each person will mine out their intended meanings, regardless of their gender. This book is intended for individuals from all faith backgrounds. Regardless of your definition of Higher Power, my hope is you will find healing here. This book is for *all* who struggle sexually and want a new life. This book is for those willing to humble themselves now before life humbles them later. This book is for those who have tasted defeat and are unwilling to stay down.

This is not a book to be read and forgotten. The stories and strategies herein must be applied for change to occur. This book is far from a quick fix. It is about the challenge of change. This book is about **mindset, mastery, and mission.**

In **Part One** we will examine necessary *mindsets* for successful recovery. Here you will see the uselessness of passivity and the power of personal responsibility. This section will challenge you to the core. You will be called out and called up. If true, lasting change is to occur, this section will prepare you for the grueling discomfort that will lead to great future growth. Here you will find both necessary conviction and needed inspiration.

Part Two is all about *mastery*. This is not a comprehensive list of all that is needed for recovery. See this section as a series of stepping stones. It provides the guidance that will get you going in the right direction. Many necessary lessons can only be learned through the process of practice. Yet without these initial directions, deep recovery will remain difficult and elusive.

Part Three is about living for a *mission*. Here you will see that recovery from sexual addiction is about much more than stopping unwanted behavior. It is about *lasting* pleasure and purpose. It is about being free to live and love fully. It is about using your dreams and talents to enrich yourself, others, and the world. This section is all about the ripple effects of living in alignment. May it inspire you to live a bigger and bolder life.

This book is much like a field manual. I recommend reading it initially from start to finish, making mental and written notes of the *Essential Mindsets*, *Skills to Master*, and M*issions to Accomplish* listed at the beginning of each chapter. The abundance of tasks may feel overwhelming at first. The truth is, there is a lot to learn, requiring a plethora of practice. So, I've crafted a plan that I call *Your Recovery Roadmap*, found at the end of the book.

The *Roadmap* is a 52-week guide to practically applying the material in a recommended order. Using the *Recovery Roadmap* in conjunction with the two indispensable ingredients of a skilled sexual addiction therapist and a sexual addiction recovery program, will add personalized guidance and structure, skyrocketing recovering addicts toward success. It should be noted that throughout this handbook the terms *sex addict*, *sexual addict*, and *pornography addict* can be used interchangeably.

Throughout this book I draw from personal experience, research, and what has helped others. It is an uncommon guide in that it is both a series of articles and a compilation of creative writing. As I've progressed through my recovery, I've cultivated a gift with words that sprouted in my childhood. This was the result of reconnecting with myself and being infused with the encouragement of others — both inherent experiences in true recovery.

Similarly, I believe you too will grow in authenticity and inspiration as you learn the art of connection and heal from life's hurts. Out of your recovery will come your contribution. Out of your pain will come your purpose.

The time for healing is now. Hesitation is a hindrance. Don't wait for all the *right* feelings, circumstances, or stars to align before choosing action. Set your sails for a new course. What lies ahead is uncertain, but is certainly superior to a life ruled by regrets.

Will you join me on the path of passionate recovery?

If your answer is "Yes," then let's begin.

Part I
Mindset

The essential element that prepares us for either success or failure in recovery is mindset. Our mindset determines how we respond to all of life's challenges. Our beliefs fuel our behavior. Our attitudes inform our actions.

Sexual addicts often remain stuck in specific cycles of thinking that make the prospect of change appear impossible. Why would someone choose such self-destructive thinking? Most of our mindset is molded through our life experiences. So often the thinking that keeps us feeling most trapped was formed in our past and reinforced through suffering. Our traumas taught us; we were trained through our pain.

When we are deep in our addiction, our mindset maintains self-destructive momentum. Carnes' "core beliefs"[6] are mindsets that keep sexual addicts stuck in shame, isolation, and disconnection. These false core beliefs are:

1) I am bad and unworthy
2) I am unlovable
3) I cannot depend on others to meet my needs
4) My highest need is sex

New mindsets must be learned and implemented for lasting changes to occur. Specific mindsets that stoke the fires of successful recovery are introduced at the beginning of each chapter of this Mindset section. Here are the *Essential Mindsets* of recovery presented in Part One:

<u>*Essential Mindset #1*</u>: *Recovery from sexual addiction is difficult, possible, and worth the effort.*

<u>*Essential Mindset #2*</u>: *Past pain that made me vulnerable to addiction must be addressed for healing to occur.*

Essential Mindset #3: Sexual addiction is serious, requiring my immediate attention.

Essential Mindset #4: I will give up everything that hinders long-term recovery.

Essential Mindset #5: As I recover from my sexual addiction, I will connect with a greater mission.

Essential Mindset #6: I take full responsibility for my past, present, and future choices.

Essential Mindset #7: Permanent sobriety is always possible.

Essential Mindset #8: Lust is a lie and never satisfies.

Essential Mindset #9: I will not objectify others, using them addictively.

Essential Mindset #10: I will not exchange one addiction for another.

Essential Mindset #11: Love is the antidote of lust; healing happens through connection.

Essential Mindset #12: I will learn to have a healthy relationship with my sexuality, rather than using it addictively.

Essential Mindset #13: My partner is worth my best recovery efforts.

Essential Mindset #14: I deserve healing and wholeness.

Essential Mindset #15: I will grow in self-love, responding with care when I experience emotional pain.

Essential Mindset #16: I will not engage in friendly conversation with my Evil Genius but will maintain an attitude of opposition, looking for ways to throw it under the bus.

Essential Mindset #17: I will maintain my recovery momentum by actively opposing passivity and fueling my passion.

Essential Mindset #18: Rather than doing as little as possible, I will do as much as necessary to recover.

Essential Mindset #19: I will find my inspiration for recovery and connect with it daily.

As we know by now, attitudes are not easily altered. Change does not materialize simply through the mere choice to make it so. It is a learning process. The acquisition of information will precede new action. We must earn our Doctoral degree, so to speak, in recovery.

This section is a starting line. It provides both essential concepts and recommended roads where necessary lessons can be learned. Here, your mindset will be challenged and, if you are open, expanded. Remember, you may initially resist the mindsets most essential to your deepest and most long-term healing. Also, it is possible that some needed attitudes will only be attained through more arduous adventures (such as therapy).

When we allow ourselves to be inspired by the influence of others who have been there, exposing ourselves continually to honorable ideas, we will gradually gain the crucial mindset of a champion. As our minds are renewed, our hearts will be transformed.[7] We will see with new and open eyes.

—■———■—

CHAPTER I

My Path Out of Porn Addiction: A Therapist's Journey[8]

Essential Mindset #1: Recovery from sexual addiction is difficult, possible, and worth the effort.

Essential Mindset #2: Past pain that made me vulnerable to addiction must be addressed for healing to occur.

I came into the world surrounded by love. Kind to animals and humans alike, I was a caring, imaginative, and gentle child.

Living with my loving parents and sister, none could've predicted the pain that was to come. Much of my oncoming anguish would arrive through interactions with my alcoholic, bipolar father. At times he was creative, affectionate, and fun.

Other times he inflicted psychological and religious abuse. There were seasons of both attention and absence. I felt abandoned.

Through the years, our relationship was turbulent. I longed for my father and fought for his attention. Looking back, I see he never gave me what he had never received — a secure, connected, and healthy relationship. I was primed to seek comfort outside of connection. I was a victim who was vulnerable to the allurement of addiction.

Sexual curiosity came at a young age, as did sexual self-soothing. Then, at age 12, an unexpected exposure to pornography at a friend's house changed the course of my young life. The image I viewed that night is forever burned in my brain.

I was a shy yet ambitious adolescent, excelling in school, service, and scouting. My newfound interest in pornography first developed into a habit, growing gradually into a self-destructive force that bound me with secrecy and shame. I mastered sneakiness. Like any addict, I was skilled at finding my drug and covering my tracks. Some of my sexual excursions were at the expense of others. Those memories are laden with lasting shame.

In my late teen years, my addiction escalated, paralleling increased internal pain. I didn't know it then but those were traumatizing times for me. After acquiring an undeserved inheritance from his deceased parents, my dad's deepest downfall began. He was hostile, manipulative, and suicidal. Eventually he lost it all and I sought to save him from the horrors of homelessness.

At times my dad would just disappear. I found myself overcome with fear, scouring the streets until I found him dazed with drunkenness. Our deepest connections came on those long drives to Detox. I believed he would die if I didn't save him. In the end, I never did. He was devoured by the dangers of the streets; a victim of violence, he would never be the same.

The advent of the internet opened Pandora's Box for all porn addicts. I was no exception. I shared my struggles with my closest friends yet could not shake my shameful double life. When I finally told my mom about a dominating addiction that required professional treatment, she was shocked. I was 24 years old.

March 16, 2004 was the night of my *last hurrah*, my final fling with pornography and masturbation. The next day, I drove out of town for four days of intensive sexual addiction treatment at an *Every Man's Battle* workshop. While I attended, I sought spiritual strength. I read John Eldredge's book *Wild at Heart*, cementing my fighting commitment. When I left, I was equipped with tools and a tenacious attitude. I took responsibility for my healing. I steadfastly applied what I learned. I trained my eyes to evade lust. I began using boundaries to minimize triggers. Faithfully attending my recovery group, I learned the art of accountability calls.

I started practicing healthy habits and attending personal therapy. My therapist focused on my father-related pain more than my porn use. Confused at the time, I later realized why I needed this. Together, we courageously walked into my wounds. Deep healing required attending to the driving force of my addiction, the hurts in my heart. Without going back, I could not go forward.

Though it was one of the toughest tasks of my life, I took the risk of trusting God and others. This marked a new path in my recovery journey.

Opportunities to help others opened up. Deciding to make a career and calling out of sexual addiction work, I moved to

Fresno, California, where I earned my Master's degree in Marriage and Family Therapy. My senior paper was entitled *Protecting Children from the Path of Pornography*. After graduation, I became certified as a Sexual Addiction Treatment Provider (SATP) and went on to work with a local LifeSTAR outpatient treatment program. Once licensed, I became the program's Clinical Director.

There I have the opportunity to help sexual addicts, their partners, and young people as they recover from sexual addiction and its detrimental effects. I now train therapists to do sexual addiction treatment through the SATP program from which I graduated. I aim to be a voice for those silently struggling, yet too ashamed to speak up. Sometimes this means talking to parents about the threats of the internet and teaching teens about the pains of porn addiction. I have grown through these experiences and I am grateful. This is all part of my purposeful path.

In recovery, I realize that the love I sought through lust was always around me. I enjoy deepening connections with God, family, and friends. I have a caring and beautiful bride of 11 years. I get to re-define the meaning of fatherhood, giving to my boys that which I never received. I'm growing to trust a Divine Daddy so different from my own. I'm increasing in affection for my pained self inside. The long line of generational addiction in my family of origin can end with me. Learning to love and be loved is the challenge of my lifetime.

My story has come full circle. I have not indulged in pornography or masturbation in over 12 years, since that fateful March evening. More importantly, I have experienced deeper healing. While this may sound like a flawless recovery, I assure you it is far from that. I have fought and failed in many ways. I still wrestle with resentment. When feeling weakened, visual lust remains my Achilles heel. Still, I do not excuse myself from this fervent fight.

Sometimes I seek out "lesser evils," soothing myself with sugar, drowning myself in distraction, working harder to win a sense of worth, and seeking attention over connection. I am aware of the ways I am vulnerable to addiction. I remain an adult child of an alcoholic, with wounds that demand both my time and attention. To maintain momentum, I must work my recovery. I continue to pursue healing for past pain, a shame-based identity, and a victim mentality. I remain accountable to many. I contend to care for myself. I, like all humans, am a person in progress. As it was in the beginning, so it remains; recovery is a one-day-at-a-time process.

Stepping into the Stigma

Sexual addicts are socially stigmatized. It seems that "those people" are labeled as lower down the ladder than other types of addicts. This judgment of how we've coped with our pain only shames us into silence and deeper isolation.

For this generation to stand a chance, we must begin bold conversations about this uncomfortable topic. I hope someday the stigma is silenced and that hooked and hurting individuals from all walks of life will feel safe enough to come forward, giving their wounds the attention that's warranted.

Leading with vulnerability, I willingly, publicly, step into the stigma. My desire is that those who read this will experience boosted belief in the hope of healing.

Reaching For You

I was once addicted to pornography. It does not define me but it does remind me. When I look at my life, my family, my friends, and my work, I'm amazed at where recovery has led me. The gifts are worth the grief. This has been the most difficult yet most rewarding path of my life and I wouldn't trade it for anything.

With the help of others, I have climbed up the steep path and out of the valley. I will continue extending my hand down to anyone brave enough to grab hold of it. I will continue using my life lessons, the science I've studied, and the strategies that have strengthened others to help anyone ready to rise up.

Will you have the boldness to believe in the hope of recovery?

Will you reach out and take this recovering rebel's hand?

When you do, your life will never be the same. Nobody can predict what adventures lie ahead for you. I can only imagine the depth of meaning and connection waiting on your personal horizon. Such is the steep path out of sexual addiction:

Frightening.

Exhilarating.

Possible.

I can attest with certainty that the view from the top is astounding, satisfying beyond words, and worth every grueling step.

CHAPTER 2

Called to Rise

Essential Mindset #3: Sexual addiction is serious, requiring my immediate attention.

Essential Mindset #4: I will give up everything that hinders long-term recovery.

Essential Mindset #5: As I recover from my sexual addiction, I will connect with a greater mission.

Recovery from sexual addiction can feel impossible. For many, it is one of the hardest addictions to overcome. Several factors complicate sexual compulsivity. These include age of first exposure to sex and pornography, extremity and frequency of acting out behaviors, presence of early abuse or trauma, and underlying disorders.

Sexual addicts in recovery have a disadvantage because our drug is always available. Can you imagine the challenge of abstinence if a chronic smoker had cigarettes attached to their body? Sexual addicts can find sensual images almost anywhere. Whenever we want to we can get a good high in our own minds. We are our own pharmacy.[9]

Dr. Patrick Carnes differentiates sexual addiction from other addictions, noting how sexuality plays on all five of the senses.[10] An alcoholic doesn't care how beautiful their beer is. The sexual addict is attentively tuned into the visual attractiveness of their lust-drug and the other senses play their part in this sexual symphony. Of course this also means that all five senses can become compelling triggers, increasing the unwelcome allure for those trying to resist temptation.

Also, sexual addiction plays on powerful neurochemicals. Used repeatedly throughout time, it can be difficult to pause this pattern. At the first sign of sobriety, some go through severe withdrawal. In this excruciating state, it is really hard not to run back to familiar highs. Additionally, when sexual experiences are sought to cope with all of life's stressors, sexual addicts do not naturally know the benefits of reaching for relational soothing or other forms of healthy coping. This can result in lengthened periods of discomfort without their drug of choice. These are some of the significant reasons why sexual addiction is so challenging to overcome.

What Will We Do?
So, what will we do with this information? Crawl into a corner and wait for the next craving? Will we continue with futile attempts that further our sense of failure? Will we simply settle for a disconnected, compulsive, and mediocre existence? We can

choose those things. But if we do, there are unforeseen and unpredictable consequences. We take great risk.

I believe those we love are worth more. We are worth more.

Are you ready to do the work of recovery, knowing that it will likely be the hardest ordeal of your life? I stand in agreement with Arnold Palmer who said that the "most rewarding things you do in life are often the ones that look like they cannot be done."[11] In the face of this seemingly impossible feat, will you have the courage to face your greatest fears and rise up?

Aching to Escape

In the Batman movie *The Dark Knight Rises,* we were introduced to a similarly difficult scenario. Alfred set the scene describing a distant pit-like prison where men were dumped to die.

It was in this pit where Bruce Wayne (Batman) was cast to waste away, while Bane, the villain, ravaged his city. Bruce's heart was set on escape. With a thick rope tied around his waist, he ascended the tall chasm. About halfway up, he reached a ledge where he could leap. In that decisive moment he flew through the air, missed the necessary hand-hold, then plummeted down to the painful end of his rope. Despite his dangerous descent, he kept training and trying, haunted by the historic moment when a child once successfully climbed up and out. This gave Bruce enough belief to persevere.

As Bruce considered the very real ramifications of remaining in the pit, he decidedly declared that he would not die in there. On the TV he saw his city going to hell in a hand basket, an angering and unacceptable reality he was determined to change.

Do you possess a motivating passion to escape the pain that is packaged with a lust-driven life? It could come from the humiliation of getting caught, the trauma of those who trust you, massive missed opportunities and denied dreams, disconnection from the Divine, damaged credibility, the continuation of generational addiction, or the nagging guilt of living an incongruent life. Maybe you have tasted some of these trials. Maybe the denial is so deep, you think you are the exception; surely *you* will escape unscathed. Why fight hard for your freedom when you can postpone it another day?

The problem with this wishful thinking is it is both unrealistic and un-motivating. I have seen so many people deny their future destruction until it was staring them dead in the face.

Rising from the Pit

One day, a blind prisoner gave Bruce the key to his puzzle, taking his efforts to the next level. He told Bruce that in order to tap into the strength to ascend beyond what he believed was possible, he needed to connect with his fear and the fight to survive. The only way this would be accomplished was making the climb like the child did, without his safety rope. Only then, the prisoner promised, would he connect with a much deeper motivating fear.

In the next scene, Bruce packed up his meager belongings. Walking up to the bottom of the dark hole, he refused the rope. The crowd gathered as he began his final climb. This time it was all or nothing. Failure would be fatal. Knowing this, Bruce ascended with a deeper determination. In a foreign language, his fellow prisoners began chanting "Rise! Rise! Rise!"

Then Bruce came to the fateful ledge where he had failed time and time again. In a moment of breath-taking silence, Bruce leaped farther than ever before. In that shocking second, he caught the ledge and pulled himself up to the next level. The crowd cheered. Shortly after, he climbed out of the darkness into a bright new day. Before leaving for his greater mission, he dropped a rope down for others who were ready to make the courageous climb themselves. He was free.

What is Your Rope?

When you think about the potential for healing from sexual addiction, what is your *rope*? Your rope represents that which feels easy, safe, or convenient but hinders real recovery. It keeps you comfortable enough that you never connect with the determined passion to defy all odds, creating a liberated life of lasting change.

A sexual addict's rope could be their unwillingness to give up all forms of lust. This may mean an external commitment to eradicate public acting out while internally staying in a state of sensual intoxication. Another rope could be isolation. This could entail stopping addictive behavior without replacing it with healing connection. Avoidance of pain is another potential rope. This could lead someone to avoid exposing infected inner wounds to a therapist, propel a passive attitude, increase dishonesty and the protection of shameful secrets, or weaken one's willingness to wrestle through withdrawal.

All of these strategies put on the appearance of healing but will inevitably lead to false starts and failed attempts. Without the surrender of such ropes, recovery will remain surface level. Thorough transformation will not occur.

Think about it: What ropes are restricting *your* recovery? Write them down.

Made for a Mission

As you consider surrendering your restrictive ropes, imagine what meaningful mission is worth pursuing beyond your pit. I believe each of us was created to contribute. Every person has a purpose. When one of us is absent from life's arena due to disconnection and addiction, we all suffer. But when one warrior courageously climbs out of their pit, they are transformed in the process. They grow in love for others and themselves. They wish for a better world. Self-esteem is strengthened. Boldness is bolstered. Ability to rest in the hands of a Higher Power is restored. Faith in community comes to fruition. In such a state of mind, they are readied to make a ripple effect. Rising from the pit, they are prepared to meet their greatest potential. If you were free to fulfill your highest purpose, what would you pursue? Meditate on your mission. Allow future adventures to fuel present resolve.

Imagining the freedom of the future, I believe you will find the courage to make the climb of your life. It is true that recovery from sexual addiction is painfully difficult. But Bruce Wayne will tell you that leaving behind the comforts of the rope to re-engage in the adventure is both honorable and heroic. As you look up and begin placing one hand over another, those of us who have climbed and conquered are cheering you on. Collectively we call out, "Rise! Rise! Rise!"

You can do this. This is the steep path of least regrets, a path to be proud of.

This is the courageous climb up to life after lust.

CHAPTER 3

Don't Be a Victim to Sexual Addiction[12]

Essential Mindset #6: I take full responsibility for my past, present, and future choices.

Essential Mindset #7: Permanent sobriety is always possible.

You are not helpless against your sexual addiction. Neither am I. Yet we so often act as if there is nothing we can do in this battle against temptation, going with the flow rather than fighting for our freedom.

To make matters worse, many remain in a state of blame for their behavior. From the beginning of time, it seems we humans have voraciously sought out someone or something to hold responsible for personal choices. Heaven forbid we look in the mirror and ask "What choices led me here?" or "What choices can I make now?"

Instead, we often remain in victim mode, scanning the landscape for reasons why we *had* to give in or reasons why we can't change.

If we look for excuses to act out sexually, we will find them. I hear them all the time...

"I don't get enough sex."

"I just have a high libido."

"I'm on vacation."

"I was alone and tired."

"I don't know how to get free."

"Everyone does it."

"The Devil made me do it."

It seems that we'll blame any feeling, person, circumstance, time of day, impulse, or desire for our choice to give in.

I know this mentality all too well. Most of my life I camped out in the valley of a victim mindset. It did not serve me, but instead made me feel stuck when I wasn't. But I credit much of my success in my personal fight against sexual addiction to choosing to no longer act helpless against my addiction or other contributing factors. This lesson did not come cheaply or easily. I invested much time and money to acquire it. The secret of my success is taking personal responsibility for my recovery. When I remind myself that I can't *change* all of my circumstances but I can *choose* most of my responses to them, I regain my power. Fighting against victim mentality is a daily battle for me. I believe this is some of the most significant work for anyone in active recovery.

What keeps us feeling stuck is our addiction to our excuses. Sadly, most do not passionately pursue healing until life "makes" them do it. They face painful consequences of potential divorce, court involvement, job loss, and countless other wake-up calls. While these things motivate momentary change, it will not remain without continual choices. How could it, when they base their recovery on their circumstances not on their decisions? In these cases, once the situation cools down, so does their resolve.

I write this at the risk of sounding insensitive. I really do care about the pain of others. I know many truly are victims of abuse and injustice, and I do not want to downplay the sadness of those situations. I have deep wounds of my own. From moods to mental illness, many of us struggle in many ways. But if we're not careful, we can begin to blame these things for the life we are choosing. This mindset is a trap. These life experiences are not reasons to relinquish responsibility. We still have choices. We can live a life of victimhood and justification, but these mindsets will never lead to healing.

I share this perspective because I know many people act helpless against their sexual addiction in ways that do not serve them. I don't say this to contradict the concept of powerlessness presented in 12-Step based programs. I admit, as addicts there are predictable situations when we'll swerve into the auto-pilot of addiction. For those caught in that cycle, it can feel hopeless. But if we fully acknowledge our weaknesses, can we not proactively work hard at seeking help and searching for solutions?

For example, if there are situations when we feel powerless against pornography, why would we allow ourselves unfiltered and open access to it if we are truly willing to be free from it? Again, if we know our day will be packed with distractions and difficulties that could trigger addictive thinking, we can ground ourselves in the strength of our Higher Power and call our support system. If we spot an attractive person we're tempted to objectify, we can take a detour with our legs or our eyes.

Knowing the circumstances and states of mind that leave us vulnerable, we can actively, mindfully use the tools of recovery to create new outcomes. When we are feeling strong, we prepare for when we will feel weak.[13] We sweat more in times of training so we can bleed less when our battles begin.[14] We learn to proactively protect ourselves by seeking the support and practicing the skills we'll need to sustain recovery success.

When we take responsibility for our recovery, we courageously acknowledge our countless choices. We can still admit our weaknesses and deficiencies but they do not mean we are helpless. We can choose to not let those keep us down. We can research alternatives. We can ask questions. We can seek support. We can choose community. We can pursue spiritual connection. We can choose to never give up.

I believe there is a way out of all temptations.[15] Yet too often we look for every possible way *into* temptation. If we believe there is always a way out, how hard will we look for it? To what lengths will we go to make sure we find it?

For those tired of getting tossed around by temptations, take a few minutes to write down honest answers to the following questions:

- How am I acting helpless against pornography, lust, and other acting-out behaviors?
- Do I *want* to change? If yes, am I *willing* to change? In other words, am I willing to do everything it takes to change?
- In what ways am I making myself vulnerable to temptation?

- What needs to change in my life to help me tap into my Higher Power's strength and the support of others?
- What are my potential blind spots and what resources will help me see the truth in these areas? (Hint: You may need to ask others about your blindspots).
- What wounds have I ignored throughout my life that are in need of my attention?
- What strengths, gifts, and abilities can I leverage in my recovery?
- Who can I reach out to for help?

When we steadfastly seek answers we will find them.[16]

Please note, this is not about blaming or shaming ourselves. Taking responsibility is about becoming empowered. It's about seeing what we did to get here and deciding what else we could do, right now. We will lack the freedom we desire in our recovery as long as we pretend that it doesn't exist.

Will you take responsibility for your recovery? When you do, the possibilities are endless. Sure, you can go on pretending you are helpless. That's your choice. But I believe you can choose a better life than that. I know I want a better life than that.

Be empowered. You are resourceful. You are creative. You have options. You are not destined to relapse. Permanent sobriety is always possible. There is so much you can do to seek and strive for healing. I challenge you to choose wisely which way you will go.

You can choose addiction or recovery, lethargy or life.

May we all choose life.[17]

CHAPTER 4

---◆-----◆---

The Lie of Lust

Essential Mindset #8: Lust is a lie and never satisfies.

Essential Mindset #9: I will not objectify others, using them addictively.

Essential Mindset #10: I will not exchange one addiction for another.

Essential Mindset #11: Love is the antidote of lust; healing happens through connection.

Essential Mindset #12: I will learn to have a healthy relationship with my sexuality, rather than using it addictively.

Victory in recovery begins with victory over lust. The sexual addict who solely focuses on abstaining from pornography, compulsive masturbation, illicit sexual encounters, or other acting out behavior does themselves a disservice if they ignore the root problem of lust. Sexual addiction is an addiction to lust. Thus, sexual sobriety necessitates abstinence from lust in all forms. This is easier said than done.

Since we need to learn to resist lust, we need to know what lust is. Surprisingly, deciding on a definition of lust is difficult. Some might say "I know it when I feel it." If we resort to a dictionary definition, lust is explained as an "intense or unbridled sexual desire."[18] When we consider the sexual addict's experience of lust, this definition is severely lacking. The sexual addict's problem is not a high libido or a zeal for sex. Their problems emerge from an unhealthy *relationship* with sex, from using sex as a drug (See the *Connected Sex* chapter for more information).

With this in mind, let's consider an experience-based explanation. This is how I define sexual lust: ***An insatiable intoxication intentionally pursued through the sexual objectification of someone***.

Let's dissect that.

Insatiable - Lust of the mind and eyes never satisfies.[19] The more we indulge, the more we desire. A view inside our brains explains this experience. Dopamine is a dominant neurotransmitter sought after in sexual addiction. Dr. Kelly McGonigal writes that "a dopamine rush doesn't create happiness itself" but alerts the brain to "the possibility of feeling good," [20] motivating people to pursue more of that feeling. Dopamine triggers anticipation in the brain but never creates satisfaction. This is a perfect description of lust. A lifetime of lust would never be enough. The lustful sensation seeker will always thirst for more.

Intoxication - When a sexual addict objectifies another, they *use* the image as a drug, experiencing a momentary pleasure *hit* or *high*. A lust *binge*, a state of a non-stop lust indulgence, leads to lustful "drunkenness,"[21] as Sexaholics Anonymous calls it.

Intentionally - When an attractive person walks into view or when a sexual thought comes to mind, this is not lust. Lust requires a willful act. The choices to look again or to entertain a fantasy are acts of lust.

Sexual - For the sexual addict, lust is an unnatural response to a natural sexual instinct. Although we are sexual beings, we were not meant to remain in a constant state of arousal. The sexual addict is unaware of this, unceasingly pursuing sexual stimulation. They may even sexualize that which is not meant to be sexual. A person performing a non-sexual act, like walking down the street, could be sexually objectified regardless of their intentions. Also, lust accompanies all forms of sexual acting-out behaviors.

Objectification - When we choose to see others or ourselves as a collection of body parts rather than human beings worthy of honor and respect, we objectify them. People do not exist solely for our sexual pleasure, but we can pretend they do. However, depending on our frame of mind, we can see an attractive person and not objectify them.

The Losses of Lust

For the sexual addict there is no *responsible* lusting. Just like an alcoholics' inability to drink without indulgence, a sexual addict cannot sample lust without wanting more.[22]

When we feel we cannot live without lust, we are down the all-consuming road of addiction. My dad used to repeatedly remind me of this progressive process, sharing how "the man takes a drink, the drink takes a drink, then the drink takes the man."[23] As St Augustine said, "the service of lust ended in habit, and habit, not resisted, became necessity."[24] Lust is both the bait and the trap. For the sexual addict, casual lusting quickly evolves into impulsive indulgence, leading to dependence and predictable self-destruction.

Those who pursue lust as a momentary solution to their pain experience more pain in the end. After moments of temporary pleasure, the user awakens to the consequences of their choices. There is always a cost to lust.

The consequences of a lust-filled life could include a continual sense of shame and deepened disconnection from self and others. Lust can taint beautiful memories. When lust escalates, it can lead to increasingly dark and deviant behaviors. As time passes, the losses of lust pile up. The high is not worth the hurt.

The Challenge of Lust-Free Living

Have you faced this reality first-hand? If you're ready to take control rather than remaining controlled, will you join me in the fight for lust-free living? If lust is your drug of choice, expect to strongly resist this invitation. If you want to experience life after lust, yet wrestle with whether the work is worth it, write down your answers to the following questions:

- Thinking about your personal history, how long have you depended on lust-filled living?
- In what ways has lust diminished your quality of life?
- How has lustful living deepened disconnections from your loved ones?
- Do lust and objectification go against your highest values? Which ones?
- Is the temporary lust high worth the long-term losses that could result?
- Despite its difficulty, are you willing to pursue the high calling of a lust-free life?

Love: The Antidote to Lust

Those courageous individuals who dare to daily surrender their desire to lust will benefit from replacing lust with love. Throughout our lives, many of us have mistaken one for the other yet lust and love are strikingly different. Lust increases appetite and love appeases it. Lust leaves us lacking and love meets our deepest needs. Understanding the contrast between love and lust, Shakespeare wrote:

> *Love comforteth like sunshine after rain, but Lust's effect is tempest after sun; Love's gentle spring doth always fresh remain, Lust's winter comes ere summer half be done; Love surfeits not, Lust like a glutton dies; Love is all truth, Lust full of forged lies.*[25]

A childhood lacking secure connection leaves us love-starved. Lust feels like the connection we need yet fails to fulfill us. Lust's connection is artificial, at best. In recovery, we learn the art of real connection. In seasons of suffering, we learn to reach for connecting comforts rather than the familiar shallow counterfeits. Genuine connection meets the need that lust seeks to fill. Love is the antidote to lust, the remedy that brings relief. Learning to truly connect is the solution that satisfies like lust never could.

You're likely wondering, *how does this pan out practically?* How will we go about replacing lust with love? The strategies are simple, yet are practiced through a lifetime of learning. On this new journey we must master the skills of self-connection, other connection, and spiritual connection. We must refuse to replace lust addiction with other distractions or addictions. Many strategies will be explained in the following pages.

As we progress in recovery, our aim advances from solely *avoiding* lust to actively *pursuing* love. Learning appropriate application of this is a process, since sexual addicts are intrinsically unaware of the concept of healthy boundaries. When someone attractive passes our path, what intentional act of love can we practice in their presence? This may mean honoring them by guiding our gaze elsewhere. It may mean acknowledging them as a person while maintaining pure motives. Silently praying for the person or wishing them well are other possibilities.[26] If we catch ourselves objectifying others, we can quickly take ownership, imagining our heartfelt apology to those we've used to fuel our addiction.[27]

Turning our attention toward those we are with, calling out to accountability, or grounding our soul in spiritual strength are other willful acts of connection amidst the trials of temptation. When feeling too weak to resist lust, we can see this as a sign of needed self and soul-care. At times, we will practice self-love by avoiding areas where we're vulnerable to wandering away from recovery commitments. If we're prone to objectifying ourselves or drinking in the lust of others, in recovery we practice self-love by honoring our appearance, seeking respectful, lust-free connections. When we set boundaries with those luring us back into lustful living, we actively love ourselves, our partners, and others lost in their own addictions.[28] Every time we choose to love when tempted to lust, we rewire our brains, strengthening our resolve to recover.

Life After Lust

Life after lust is an ideal but not an impossibility. As we learn the lust-free lifestyle, we will relish in the rewards. When I am actively resisting lust, I feel focused, strong, and aligned with my values. Defending against lust, my sexuality is not suppressed, it is directed like a laser, increasing my awareness of my wife's attractiveness. Fighting lust, I become trustworthy, both when I'm with others and when I'm alone. Battling against lust-fueled behavior, I am free to live and to love.

For those ready for recovery, it is time to abandon life under the influence of lust. It is time to lay down our cheap coping mechanisms, taking up strategies that strengthen us. As we leave lust behind, we begin to see ahead the hopeful makings of a new life. We begin to taste the unrivaled satisfaction of life after lust.

CHAPTER 5

What My Wife is Worth

Essential Mindset #13: My partner is worth my best recovery efforts.

Essential Mindset #14: I deserve healing and wholeness.

This piece was originally written for the Women of Value Quickening Conference.[29] It was published on forestbenedict.com in June of 2016. Shortly afterwards, a blogger who supports partners of sex addicts named Avalon Vic created a modified version for wives called "What I Am Worth" (see Appendix A). These pieces could be modified to fit female addicts and male partners as well.

My wife is a woman of infinite worth. Because of this, she deserves my best efforts.

She deserves a husband who only has eyes for her.

She deserves a husband in active recovery, not passively going with the flow.

She deserves a husband who reminds her that she is not to blame for his past or present choices.

She deserves a husband who actively opposes visual and mental lust in all forms, viewing it as the enemy of true intimacy.

She deserves a husband who is trustworthy, both when she is looking and when she's unaware.

She deserves a husband who seeks help when needed, remaining accountable to those who call out his greatness and strength.

She deserves a husband with the courage to face his deepest fears, inadequacies, and wounds for the sake of his healing.

She deserves a husband who learns from his mistakes, creating and communicating new plans for change.

She deserves a husband who is learning how to connect and does the hard work in spite of insecurities and inadequacies in this area.

She deserves a husband who tells the truth about his behavior and is honest when his heart wants to wander.

She deserves a husband who does whatever it takes to change whatever wounds her.

She deserves a husband who takes responsibility for his life, rather than being a victim of circumstances, feelings, or personal history.

She deserves a husband who progresses in personal growth, who is becoming the man he's told her he wants to be.

She deserves a husband who is committed to perseverance and course correction, who gets up quickly after failures.

She deserves a husband who cares for himself so that he can offer her more presence and participation in daily life.

She deserves a husband who models faith, purity, passion, and purpose to their children.

She deserves a husband who acknowledges his imperfections yet resists using them as justifications for a small life.

She deserves a husband who fights for her heart.

She deserves a husband who pursues her emotional and physical safety.

She deserves a husband who cherishes her, pursues her, and defends her.

She deserves a husband who humbly responds to her personal boundaries and listens to the pain his choices have caused.

She deserves a husband who remains patient when forgiveness and trust do not come quickly.

She deserves a husband who desires her, cutting off opportunities to seek all counterfeit connections.

She deserves a husband who nurtures her, encourages her to use her gifts, and empowers her to come alive.

She deserves a husband who supports her needs for relationships, relaxation, rest, and rejuvenation.

She deserves a husband who serves her, looking for ways to lighten her load.

She deserves a husband who is eager to invest both his time and attention.

She deserves a husband who sees her, knows her, and loves her.

She deserves a husband who reminds his wife every day that her value does not depend on her weight, her style, her sexiness or sexual availability, how she was treated as a child, or any other outside factor.

She deserves a husband who reminds her that she is beautiful and she is enough.

Her worth is innate and cannot be tarnished.

She deserves all of these things because she is a person of infinite worth.

And so am I.

CHAPTER 6

———•———

Escaping the Grip of Your Evil Genius

Essential Mindset #15: *I will grow in self-love, responding with care when I experience emotional pain.*

Essential Mindset #16: *I will not engage in friendly conversation with my Evil Genius but will maintain an attitude of opposition, looking for ways to throw it under the bus.*

As an unmarried, young adult active in my addiction, I masterfully deceived those I most loved. My best friend was no exception. Every time I slept over at his house, my mindset morphed as I slipped into my addictive alter ego. The circumstance that triggered my conniving motives was the presence of porn presented through late-night movies.

Once I was aware of them, achieving access became a game to me. My friend had the best intentions of deterring me from his dad's TV. He probably had me promise not to pursue it or removed the remote. Once, he stacked objects by the door in hopes that he would wake up when I went out to watch something. Yet, despite every tactic he attempted, my creativity rose to meet the challenge. When the lights went out, I acted asleep while my mind went to work. Getting up quietly without waking others became a highly-developed skill set. I sneakily sought to outsmart my friend, accessing my adrenaline rush and securing my addictive high. The next morning was predictable. Waking with a shame hangover, I feared the disappointed look on my friend's face. I could not bear the weighty truth that I had betrayed him.

Now, despite years of recovery, TVs remain a trigger for me. Sleeping in new situations with a TV nearby, I am often awakened by tempting voices, calling me onto that self-destructive path. They beckon me back to steal a look, explaining how I could easily get away with it. I've contrived a name for this convincing voice that calls me to creatively sneak back into lustful debauchery. I call this voice my Evil Genius.

What is the Evil Genius?
Those of us who struggle with sexual addiction know our Evil Genius well. The Evil Genius is the part of us that places inventive ideas in our minds on how to numb our pain or increase our pleasure. Our Evil Genius once served the powerful purpose of helping us survive. Its tactics helped us cope with our hurts. Sadly, the Evil Genius' attempts to help us backfired. It led us down darker paths where we did things we will forever regret. In its search for sexual soothing, our Evil Genius neglected our

long-term goals, leaving us recoiling from the consequences. It seems that the strategies of our Evil Genius gave us temporary relief but repeatedly threw us under the bus. Its attempts to comfort us left us bloodied and broken.

The Evil Genius is a pet name for *preoccupation*, which is presented in Patrick Carnes' Addiction Cycle.[30] This seemingly infinite cycle begins with the sexual addict feeling some sort of pain. Not knowing how to manage this in a healthy manner, the addict plans methods of self-medication. This preoccupation leads to rituals, which result in acting out behaviors, then shame, compounded with pain,[31] is present. To the non-addicted onlooker, it may seem obvious that preoccupation is not the solution to suffering but the hook that catches us, keeping us in it. If we don't learn how to spot preoccupation then our chances of stopping it are stunted. We must understand the tactics of our Evil Genius to stand a chance of escaping its grip.

The Top Tricks of the Evil Genius

1. **<u>Deception.</u>** There are countless lies the Evil Genius will tell to lure us into the shadows. If we find our minds describing how lust is a viable solution that will satisfy, how our behavior won't hurt anyone, or how we can keep our choices hidden, these are all deceptive inner dialogues. When we listen to minimizing assertions that our addiction isn't serious or that we can sample lust without going *all the way*, these messages feed our dangerous denial.

2. **<u>Euphoric recall.</u>** Do you ever find yourself thinking back to the good ol' days of your addiction while oblivious to the painful consequences that resulted? When memories of pleasure are devoid of the pain that was present, this is

euphoric recall.[32] The Evil Genius uses this fraudulent form of fantasy to whet our appetite to return to our disastrous addiction.

3. **Creative ideas.** When our mind imagines innovative methods of acting out our addiction, it is the workings of the Evil Genius. An inventive idea may come to our consciousness regarding pleasure in the present or we may mentally stash it for the future, giving ourselves a relapse raincheck.

If we're uncertain whether our Evil Genius is at work, we can ask ourselves the following questions:

- Am I thinking about how to *get around* a recovery boundary I've put into place?
- Am I contemplating how to *get away* with indulging lust in any form?
- Do I have any pre-planned paths into sexual curiosities that could threaten my future sobriety?
- Am I minimizing the threat of any current temptations?
- Am I imagining how much I've enjoyed my past addiction while ignoring the accompanying crisis filled consequences?

If we answer "yes" to any of these questions, our Evil Genius is dangerously close and it is time to act in our defense.

The Best Defense

1. **Don't debate.** The childhood advice "don't talk to strangers" is wise counsel when it comes to our Evil

Genius. We can acknowledge it and set a boundary, saying something like "Hello, Evil Genius. Your ideas are off the table today." Further friendly banter is the Evil Genius' bait. Our Evil Genius has a way with words; this is where it does its best work. It knows our weaknesses. It knows what lines will lure us away to lust. We can tell it the truth of how we will live but when it responds, we must turn a deaf ear. This can be difficult if we don't decipher the difference between our Evil Genius and our Wiser Self. This is one reason why we must know our commitments, aiming for daily alignment with them.

If we catch ourselves in the current of conversation, we must quickly disengage. Remaining in the mind-game of the Evil Genius, we'll find ourselves losing more the longer we play. Before we know it, we'll buy the lies, betraying our most cherished convictions. When the addiction's anesthesia wears off, we'll find ourselves deeper down the dark hole of despair than we've ever ventured before.

2. **<u>Throw it under the bus.</u>** What's required when the Evil Genius calls is immediate action. In the moment, we can ask ourselves these questions:

- What can I do right now that will end this before it starts?
- What decision will close the door and stop wasting my time contemplating this temptation? In other words, what do I need to do to throw my Evil Genius under the bus?

We can start by listing our options, mentally or in writing. Our choices will be situation specific but could include:

- Calling an accountability partner
- Reaching out to our Higher Power in prayer
- Removing ourself from the situation
- Tending to our self-care needs

Next, we must choose swiftly, before our Evil Genius tries to talk us out of it (and we're not listening to it anyway, right?). I suggest choosing an option that *turns in* or *tells on* our Evil Genius. We can do this by wrapping our struggles with words. We can say something to others such as "Part of me wants to do ___ but I am forgetting how ___ happened last time. I am committed to _____ and I need to be reminded of that." This removes the power from our secret thoughts. The phrase we commonly use in recovery work is "reach out or act out."[33] Reaching for the phone instead of reaching for the porn quickly weakens our Evil Genius because suddenly we have someone on our side.

3. **Meet our need.** One significant factor that awakens and empowers our Evil Genius is the presence of an unmet need. If we lack energy due to poor sleep habits, mismanagement of stress, the absence of exercise, or unhealthy eating, we prime our brains to impulsively seek instant gratification.[34] Often, the mere presence of our Evil Genius is the sign of a deeper problem. In response, we could internally explore it, saying, "I hear my Evil Genius telling me to start searching the internet. Is this

the sign of an unmet need? It's obvious to me that I'm physically exhausted. Instead, I'm going to lay down and take a nap. Thanks for the reminder, Evil Genius!" We can often silence our Evil Genius by simply meeting our need at hand.

4. **Pay attention to our pain.** Remember how the Addiction Cycle begins with pain? In recovery, we stop addictively *reacting* to our pain and begin lovingly *responding* to it. The pained part in us doesn't need some lust-filled distraction. It needs care and compassion. In recovery, we learn to become our own loving parent, [35] so to speak. The presence of our Evil Genius reminds us to pay attention rather than neglecting the cries of our heart.

5. **Pollute our fantasy.** When faced with euphoric recall, we can remind ourselves (or ask others to remind us) of the uncomfortable realities that accompanied our past escapist behavior.

   - What physical, emotional, and spiritual discomfort was present?
   - How did we unknowingly harm ourselves and others?
   - What else could happen? Let's think about the worst case scenarios.

This is essentially reminding ourselves, "Yes, I could indulge my addiction in unique and unprecedented ways but then I'd experience unique and unprecedented consequences." We can pop our own fantasy bubble by considering how the Evil Genius will deteriorate our relationships, our self-worth, and our potential.

6. **<u>Empower our Wiser Self.</u>** The martial art of Jujitsu is centered around using the attacker's momentum to defeat them. Similarly, when the Evil Genius calls, consider practicing something meaningful. When the Evil Genius tempts us to turn to lust to just survive, we can do something that enlists our Wiser Self, helping us thrive. Whether we tend to our wounds or attend to our loved ones, what was meant to worsen our situation can be repurposed to improve it.

Putting it Into Practice

Recently, when I was out of town, I fell asleep on the couch while putting my son to sleep. Sleeping in the vicinity of a TV was not problematic until my Evil Genius woke me at 3am. I contemplated the creative ideas my Evil Genius presented to me. It showed me how the odds were in my favor for turning on the TV without waking anyone up.

I then realized my immediate risk. I started some recovery related reading, hoping to sway myself back to my stronger self. It wasn't working. I tried journaling. As I wrote, I became aware that distraction was not the answer. I needed to sleep but was unable to, against the backdrop of my Evil Genius' dominating ideas. I considered how I could throw him under the bus before he did the same to me. If I lingered much longer, I knew his betraying intentions would soon lead my addictive actions.

I began throwing my Evil Genius under the bus by waking up my wife. I asked her if we could trade places. Without question, she got up and went out on the couch in front of the TV. I lay down feeling safe from the temptations at hand.

Suddenly, our little one cried out, "Mommy!" As my wife returned, I knew I was headed back out to the couch. In that moment, I imagine my Evil Genius dusting himself off, preparing for his victory dance. But to his surprise, I leveraged his momentum against him, landing him swiftly back under the bus. I cemented my victory by placing both the TV's remote and my glasses by my wife's bed, closing the door. Feeling free from the power of my Evil Genius, I crashed on the couch. I slept soundly the rest of the night.

The next day, I shared the story of struggle with my wife. She thanked me for noble choices made in the silent hours of the night.

When it comes to my Evil Genius, it's till death do us part. Truthfully, my Evil Genius lives in me. I must never underestimate his power to persuade me with cunningly creative words. The better I get at spotting him, the stronger I'll get at stopping him. My Evil Genius is right here, but right now I respond in active opposition. It's my Evil Genius or me. One of us is going under that bus. And it ain't gonna be me.

CHAPTER 7

—◆———◆—

Defending Against Prelapse:
From Passivity to Passion[36]

***Essential Mindset #17:** I will maintain my recovery momentum by actively opposing passivity and fueling my passion.*

Time and time again, I have watched the sprint of early recovery dissipate into a stroll of passivity. Initial passion for recovery, often fueled by crisis or catastrophe, pushes people powerfully forward. Yet, unless this momentum is maintained, addicts will gradually revert to a risky state of inactivity. Dr. Patrick Carnes, leading expert in the field of sexual addiction recovery, points out this pattern of heightened acting-out behavior in the *second* six months of recovery.[37] Whether it is early on or years down the road, it is clear that regardless of the intensity of early recovery commitments, anyone can wane in their resolve. This half-hearted, mindless, and dangerous state that precedes relapse is best described as *prelapse.*

In one of the climactic scenes of *The Hobbit: The Battle of Five Armies,* we see a meaningful metaphor for *prelapse.* When Thorin ferociously fought his evil adversary Azog on the ice, he appeared to drown his enemy in the watery depths. Moments after sinking into the chilling, dark lake, Thorin's stunned opponent re-surfaced face-up below the sheet of ice. Seconds slid by as Thorin peered down, staring from a seemingly safe distance, in a docile and dazed attitude of passivity. Even after his enemy's eyes closed, he stayed still. His lack of action precipitated a sword swiftly stabbed through his shoe. Then the battle was fiercely re-engaged. He eventually killed his nemesis, but not without serious personal cost. Much pain was avoidable, had Thorin only seen the signs and acted accordingly.

As these images settle in your mind's eye, I urge you to ask yourself the following questions regarding your own recovery:

- In what ways am I passive, in a state of *prelapse?*
- How is denial adding to my lack of passion in my recovery?
- Have I become lazy in practicing the necessary self-care for maintaining my recovery?
- What am I doing well in my recovery?
- Am I practicing patterns of disconnection in my relationships with my Higher Power, myself, and with my support network?
- In what ways am I walking on *thin ice* in my recovery?
- In what ways am I lying to myself about my current commitment to the long road of recovery?

- What growth am I resisting in my recovery?
- What are the next bold steps in my recovery?
- Am I committed to taking the necessary action steps to change, as I become aware of my progress or lack thereof?

Consider revisiting these honest questions on a regular basis. You do not need to relapse to take time for this necessary self-examination. Right now may be the best time to seek awareness and consider action steps, before complacency leads to casualties. Remember too that the state of *prelapse* can be extremely triggering for partners of addicts. A passive state of mind reminds them of the seasons that led to their greatest losses. If these reflective questions alert you to the reality that your passion is waning, there is no time like the present to humbly course correct and work on reinvigorating your passion.

From Passivity to Passion
I have found that one of the most difficult tasks of recovery is moving from passivity to passion. Even more difficult for sexual addicts in recovery is maintaining passionate momentum. For many, this may feel impossible. While it is true that nobody is perfectly passionate, taking responsibility when our resolve is receding reminds us that we can proactively refuel our passion reserves.

If you find yourself in a state of *prelapse*, feeling stuck in passivity in your recovery, here are six suggestions for re-igniting your passion:

1. **Write out your reasons (remember why you started).** Take a few minutes to write down ten negative consequences that will result from a *passive* attitude in

your recovery. Then, write down ten positive benefits that will result from a *passionate* attitude in your recovery. Reading these lists (and adding to them) daily can powerfully propel you out of denial. You have significant reasons for passionately pursuing your recovery and there is power in remembering them.

2. **Imagine a better future.** Take a few minutes to connect with yourself in the future. Visualize yourself in ten years, imagining a future created by a *passionate* recovery (effects on relationships, view of self, and addiction). Practicing this tool daily can lead you closer to the future you hope to create.

3. **Clarify your purpose.** Create a recovery focused mission statement. Write: "In my recovery journey I am committed to..." then create your own paragraph based on your values. For example:

"Learning how to connect with others. I will pursue my recovery with passion and fight against passivity. I will not allow addiction to rob me of my dreams and unique contributions to the world. I will remain accountable and honest. With my Higher Power's help, I will lean into the discomfort of change, maintaining healthy habits, I will persevere through the pain, believing that the life of recovery will be deeply meaningful and rewarding."

Print out your statement and put it somewhere you will see it often. As you experience increased freedom, you can begin to see the bigger picture, that you are healed for a purpose.

4. **Recruit accountability.** Whether you meet online or face-to-face, there is power in intentional community, encouragement, and connection. Being around inspired individuals who are also committed to passionate and healthy living will pull you toward the life you want to live.

5. **Inspire yourself, often.** Find quotes, affirmations, music, and messages that inspire you. Collect that which uplifts you most now. Then, continually listen and look for fresh inspiration. Consider rehearsing daily the following messages (or ones that motivate you):

"Today, I take responsibility for my mindset, connection/disconnection from others, my self-care, and how I manage my triggers."

"The more I sweat in training, the less I'll bleed in battle."[38]

"Do not wait to strike till the iron is hot, but make it hot by striking."[39]

6. **Commit.** Ask yourself this: What is the next level of my recovery?

Scheduling self-care?
Getting an accountability partner?

Starting an exercise routine?

Installing filtering or accountability software (cutting off easy access)?

Achieving your first year of sobriety?

Using the tools provided here, it is my hope that you will experience a new level of growth as you pursue greater goals.

Proactively defending against *prelapse* will take continual effort. But those who courageously wrestle forward will experience both victory and the satisfaction of knowing they battled fervently and did not give up. This is the heroic journey of successful recovery.

CHAPTER 8

———•———

From Under the Rock[40]

Essential Mindset #18: Rather than doing as little as possible, I will do as much as necessary to recover.

Essential Mindset #19: I will find my inspiration for recovery and connect with it daily.

The true story of Aron Ralston's near-death experience in a canyoneering accident was vividly portrayed in the Academy Award nominated film *127 Hours*. The movie depicted Aron's outdoor adventure, which came to a halt when his fall into a steep crevice loosened a massive rock. As he and the rock fell, it tumbled onto his arm, pinning him down. The account of Aron's struggle to free himself provides a fitting metaphor for recovery from sexual addiction. Just as Aron was pinned under an 800-pound boulder, sexual addicts find themselves trapped under the weight of an immobilizing force.

With deadly consequences in the balance, how does someone conjure up the necessary strength, endurance, and fighting passion to escape? This question is essential as sexual addicts begin the healing journey.

Beginning Efforts

In the film, when Aron found himself trapped, he turned his efforts toward dislodging the rock. He tried to chip at it with his knife, angrily pushed against it, and even constructed a pulley system as another creative attempt. Similar to the addict who implements whichever tricks he can to outsmart his drive to seek out unhealthy sexual experiences, these efforts led only to frustration. So often, the recovery process begins with the addict doing as little as possible, rather than as much as necessary. Rather than running to health, they cautiously crawl away from their sickness, seemingly as slowly as possible.[41]

The denial that drives that mentality gradually diminishes with the increasing recognition that the *rock* of addiction is not budging. As described in the *Big Book* of AA, "half measures availed us nothing. We stood at the turning point."[42]

The sexual addict has many challenging experiences under their rock. Feeling stuck, unsure of the possibility of escape, can lead to an array of uncomfortable emotions such as anger, despair, loneliness, sadness, helplessness, and hopelessness. If this were a scraped knee, the remedy would be obvious and simple. But the circumstance a sexual addict sits in has a hidden and complex solution. The way to freedom from this trap is mysterious and frightening.

When faced with seemingly insurmountable odds, Aron gradually realized that his pathway to freedom would be agonizing, requiring the amputation of his arm. The sexual addict faces a similar dilemma; in successful recovery they must submit to the painful removal of a significant part of them.

Though it may be difficult for some to understand, a sexual addiction has sentimental value. In fact, for many it has served as a long-term source of comfort, enjoyment, and escape. Though the consequences of this pattern are destructive, the sexual addiction has served a purpose, providing a coping mechanism throughout life's trials. So, saying goodbye to the addiction is essentially severing a close relationship.

Making Necessary Cuts

Watching Aron begin to slice his arm was excruciating. Skin, muscle, bone; nothing escaped his dull, army-knife blade. Everything separating Aron from his freedom was removed. Similarly, recovering from a sexual addiction requires many uncomfortable "cuts." These choices may include **personal stretching**, such as:

- Walking into treatment
- Disclosing secret and shame-inducing behaviors
- Acknowledging consequences

Varying **behavioral changes** may be necessary, such as:

- Implementing skills for resisting temptation
- Choosing to limit access to certain conveniences, entertainment, or situations

- Practicing new self-care habits

Challenges of **relational growth** will likely be required, such as:

- Learning to be honest, vulnerable, and self-compassionate
- Learning how to emotionally connect with others
- Learning how to create safety for a traumatized partner
- Accepting help and care from others
- Growing in relationship with a Higher Power

Emotional challenges can be expected, such as:

- Learning how to acknowledge, access, express, and care for emotions rather than numbing them
- Looking at underlying issues resulting from painful past losses or traumas
- Enduring the slowness of the entire process

The recovery experience is not identical for everyone. What will be consistent is the requirement of great sacrifice.

The Frightening Path Ahead

Intimidating, isn't it? One might wonder, if recovery from sexual addiction is such a massive and life-altering experience, why submit to the process? Aron's ultimatum of life versus death was clearer than the choices a sexual addict faces. Certainly there is the choice to seek help or remain hidden in the comfort of the shadows, in the companionship of pain and shame. It is a draining, enslaving existence. Still, it is what the addict knows. And often the fear of walking into the light, uncertain of the responses of others and terrified of facing their inner emotional turmoil, burdens addicts like a ball and chain.

Under the addict's rock they are suffering as they experience deterioration of their relationships, selves, and souls. The prospect of escape is hopeful in theory but actually choosing that path takes a tremendous amount of courage and motivation.

Awakening Passion

Aron was ready to die under the rock until he found deeper inspiration. His fighting passion was finally stirred by a powerful love. In what seemed like his last hours, he saw a vision of his future son. In the film, as Aron watched himself playing with this yet unborn boy, he smiled, tears filling his eyes. This potent experience awakened in Aron a hope, determination, and fervor that was previously absent.

As Aron undertook his own amputation, there was no doubt that he believed there was more to his life than dying under that rock. He found his reason to fight.

The sexual addict must conjure up an intense passion for freedom for healing to occur. They must determine their *why*. This means finding reasons that stir in them a compelling desire to leap from their realm of comfort, embracing the possibility of a better life. This can start with looking through images of their partner, their children, or their heroes. It may include envisioning a yet unfulfilled dream or pondering values that inspire them. That reason plays a foundational role. The key to Aron's freedom was found in the visualization of the beautiful life to come. More so, the love for his future son was a force that was previously untapped. And it was that greater power that energized him to do the seemingly impossible.

Daily Inspiration

There are many strategies a sexual addict can utilize to devise their necessary, daily inspiration. The following strategies may be helpful for sexual addicts to use at set times of the day and when undergoing moment to moment temptations or challenges:

- Reading a paragraph from a book, a quote, a scripture passage, a letter written to themselves, or their list of motivating reasons to be free
- Listening to a specific song or playlist that grounds them in their spiritual beliefs, feelings of closeness to family, their true identity, a future vision, and an uncompromising attitude
- Watching movie clips that arouse motivating values and a fighting mentality
- Praying/meditating to foster feelings of connection with a Higher Power and a sense of greater purpose
- Holding symbols of recovery

Another excellent way to tap into that greater power and motivation is through the connection with others who are fighting similar battles, whether through groups, retreats, or other experiences. There is something deeply motivating about spending time within a culture or community of others committed to recovery. Powerful too is the experience of making phone calls to tap into the strength of another, connect emotionally, and mutually encourage one another.

When a person in recovery practices whatever infuses them with the power they need to fight for their freedom, the recovery process is made visible at a level never before witnessed.

The Hope of Freedom

In his book *Between a Rock and a Hard Place* Aron Ralston described the most powerful experience of his life,[43] the instant he and his arm abruptly parted company. He wrote, "A crystalline moment shatters, and the world is a different place. Where there was confinement, now there is release. Recoiling from my sudden liberation, my left arm flings downcanyon, opening my shoulders to the south, and I fall back against the northern wall of the canyon, my mind is surfing on euphoria. As I stare at the wall where not twelve hours ago I etched 'RIP OCT 75 ARON APR 03,' a voice shouts in my head: I AM FREE!"[44] In recovery, the same opportunity presents itself. Just as Aron traded his arm for his new life, recovery means trading the old for the new. Losing much, gaining more.

The movie ended informing the audience that Aron's vision became his reality; he was married and had a son. Then, real images of Aron living his life flashed across the screen. Alive. Well. Loved. Armless. If you asked Aron if his current life was worth sacrificing a significant part of him, I believe he would emphatically say it was. Certainly his son would agree.

It is an honorable step of courage to seek treatment for a sexual addiction. Sadly, there are too many who resort to living a life as a victim to their addiction, holding tightly to the only life they know, however desolate and lonely it may be under their rock. When someone seeks help, they are no longer isolated as they pursue the new life of recovery. They are met with a host of helpers who can gently guide them through the painful process, providing many resources and much support to help them take the necessary steps.

Life Awaits

May we all on this journey to wholeness be willing to fight with determination the battles before us, however fear-inducing and difficult they may be, knowing that something better awaits us on the other side. There will be times when relapse seems like saving grace, but we must realize that in those moments of discomfort, there is relief for those who reach out and push through.

In light of Aron's endeavor and the one before us, may we remember that many have gone through this life-altering surgery, separating themselves from the source of their greatest suffering.[45] They did the difficult work of laying to rest that which was most familiar. Looking ahead, they ventured up and out of their dark canyon, climbing into the hopeful light of a new life.[46] Remembering those who have ascended out of sexual addiction, may we daily seek and summon our strength and support, that we may one day join those who decisively declare "I am free!"

Part 2

Mastery

In his book *Mastery*, George Leonard shares these wise words: "At the heart of it, mastery is practice. Mastery is staying on the path."[47]

Mastery is the foundation of recovery. It is the opposite of what we would wish for. As addicts, we long for a quick fix to our inner anguish and hedonistic habits. We want to achieve our sobriety goals. We want to see the destructive results of our behavior disappear. What we don't really want is to push through the discomfort of today. We want to pretend the rules of limited time and energy do not apply to us.

Yet, there is no lasting progress without practice. Brain researcher Dr. Lara Boyd explains that "The primary driver of change in your brain is your behavior."[48] Boyd shares that putting in the hard work of practice is the foundation of learning. This is helpful when what we're practicing is positive, but destructive if we practice that which adds to our pain.[49]

This is where *mastery* comes in. Here, we learn the necessary skills, make a plan, then execute it. Daily. When we know that today's greatest goal is to *practice*, we become focused on the immediate journey rather than the distant destination. This will be a slow, intentional process. Much like learning to walk, we will stumble and fumble around. It is important to set hopeful yet realistic expectations for transformation. Dr. Jonice Webb writes that change is not linear but "comes in fits and starts. Two steps forward, one step back. The real key is to just keep working through the backward steps, consistently and persistently, until you take another step forward."[50] Recovery is all about course correction, not perfection. Through practice, we condition our minds and hearts. Through practice, we become the best we can be.

Most addicts are *masters* of secrecy, self-criticism, self-neglect, pain avoidance, and disconnection. In recovery, we gradually *let go* of these unhealthy, unhelpful practices and *grab hold* of life-giving ones. We don't just learn new methods of self-medication or distraction.

In successful recovery, we become *masters* of honesty, self-compassion, self-care, pain management, and connection. In recovery, we master ourselves, our emotions, and our responses to our circumstances. Though it will take a lifetime to master all of the recovery skills that makeup long-term recovery, here are the fundamental *Skills to Master* presented in this section:

Skill to Master #1: Achieving long-term sobriety

Skill to Master #2: Humbly reaching for help

Skill to Master #3: Caring for those wounded by my addiction

Skill to Master #4: Working cooperatively with a sexual addiction therapist

Skill to Master #5: Learning to trust my Higher Power

Skill to Master #6: Protecting myself internally and externally

Skill to Master #7: Disclosing to my partner my acting out history with the help of a trained professional

Skill to Master #8: Learning to connect in the context of a recovery group

Skill to Master #9: Learning to connect through a same-gender accountability relationship

Skill to Master #10: Consistent and effective self-care

Skill to Master #11: Healthy self-soothing and relaxation

Skill to Master #12: Shame management

Skill to Master #13: Self-connection

Skill to Master #14: Self-compassion

Skill to Master #15: Emotional regulation (managing pain and emotion)

Skill to Master #16: Minimizing self-criticism

Skill to Master #17: Self-forgiveness

Skill to Master #18: Rising quickly from perceived failures

Skill to Master #19: Seeking and sustaining inner peace

Skill to Master #20: Changing my present behavior as I connect with my future self

Skill to Master #21: Learning to emotionally connect with my partner

Skill to Master #22: Practicing a healthy, connected sexuality

Skill to Master #23: Connecting with my values

Skill to Master #24: Prioritizing important relationships

Skill to Master #25: Learning to pay attention to my children, fostering deeper connection

Skill to Master #26: *Maintaining recovery structure and self-care over the holidays*

Skill to Master #27: *Maintaining recovery structure and self-care on vacation*

Skill to Master #28: *Making worthy memories*

Skill to Master #29: *Learning to have fun apart from addiction*

Skill to Master #30: *Connecting with my reasons for fighting for my recovery*

Skill to Master #31: *Preparing for potential temptations*

Skill to Master #32: *Connecting with the legitimate needs driving my addictive cravings*

Skill to Master #33: *Learning to ask for what I need*

Skill to Master #34: *Practicing the recovery principle of "one day at a time"*

There's no question this list is lengthy. Much time must be invested to experience long-term recovery gains. Growing in all of these areas is our life's work. As long as we have breath, the opportunity is ours to build something beautiful out of the wreckage left in the wake of our addiction. After consistently practicing that which is most beneficial to us, we find we are different and we are free.

CHAPTER 9

Twelve Porn Free Years: The Secrets of My Success

Skill to Master #1: Achieving long-term sobriety

This piece was originally published on March 17, 2016 on forestbenedict.com, in celebration of a significant sobriety date.

This past year I reached a significant sobriety date: 12 years free from pornography use. This was especially significant because it mirrored the 12 previous years I was enslaved to pornography.

For the sake of personal reflection and to give back to those who are struggling, I have compiled the top 12 lessons and the top 12 recovery skills I've learned from those 12 years of transformation (in no particular order). Here they are:

Lessons
1. Connection is the opposite of addiction.[51]
2. Without going back, I cannot go forward.
3. Successful recovery requires 100 percent Me and 100 percent my Higher Power.
4. Education is empowering.
5. Daily self-care habits are the foundation of recovery.
6. Discomfort and pain are part of the process.
7. Recovery is worth the sacrifices of convenience and temporary pleasure.
8. Nobody recovers alone.
9. Love satisfies what lust never will.
10. My recovery is not progressing if I learn to be sober yet self-neglectful.
11. Recovery means learning to trust.
12. Out of my pain comes my purpose.

Recovery Skills
1. Learning to reach out to others in moments of temptation and emotional turmoil.
2. Learning to connect deeply with my Higher Power.
3. Learning to connect deeply with others (accountability, romantic partner, family, friends).
4. Learning to connect in a group.
5. Learning self-connection (including self-compassion).
6. Letting go of all forms of lust.
7. Habitual self-care.
8. Reaching out to professional help when needed.

9. Practicing play, laughter, fun, and relaxation.
10. Managing shame.
11. Taking full responsibility for my choices.
12. Finding daily inspiration.

When you look over these lists, which lessons and skills are your strengths?

Which ones are your weaknesses?

Which ones are you excited about?

Which ones fill you with fear?

What would you add to these lists?

Are you wasting time on things not on these lists that are not working for you?

Which ones are you most resisting? What if the ones you were most adamantly resisting were the keys to your greatest growth?

As you might imagine, these lessons and skills cannot be learned overnight. Most of them cannot be learned in isolation or without knowledgable help. But as you improve in each of these areas, I believe you will find joy and satisfaction that are worth all the effort. You won't become a new person. You will become more of who you really are.[52]

CHAPTER 10

———◆———

Dear Mr. Duggar: When Sexual Secrets Surface[53]

Skill to Master #2: **Humbly reaching for help**

Skill to Master #3: **Caring for those wounded by my addiction**

Skill to Master #4: **Working cooperatively with a sexual addiction therapist**

Josh Duggar, former reality TV star from the show, "19 Kids And Counting," was among many exposed during the Ashley Madison hack in 2015. Duggar and his family were famous for upholding faith and family values on the show. This made his infidelity and association with Ashley Madison, a website dedicated to married-dating and extramarital affairs, even more shocking to the public. In Duggar's statement to the public, he admitted his hypocrisy, sharing about his secretive sexual addiction, which included pornography use and infidelity.[54] Mr. Duggar is representative of millions of people whose sexual secrets have surfaced unexpectedly. This fictional letter is addressed to Mr. Duggar but written for all who have experienced this kind of devastating discovery.

Dear Mr. Duggar,
My name is Forest and I too was once shackled by sexual addiction. I now work with the walking wounded, coaching them to crawl from the ashes of addiction into the light of new life. Please receive these words with an open heart, so that you may ascend from the valley of self-imposed suffering.

I imagine you're feeling unprecedented shame. Just days after publicly confessing hypocrisy, a secret pornography addiction, and infidelity, your betrayal booms across the internet and the gossip grows. Your confession will be among many. Following the submerged explosion, sexual secrets will soon ceaselessly rise to the surface of the public's awareness, thanks to the Ashley Madison hack that has stunned us all.

Yet, for every individual whose discretions are discovered, there are countless others who remain buried in the depths of addiction. Sadly, in their shame they stay silent. Like you, most of them won't step forward in surrender until their choices catch up with them, stabbing the backs of both them and their loved ones.

This is where you find yourself, leveled by the impact of your discovery and your disclosure. Mr. Duggar, I urge you to open your eyes to the opportunity before you.

These suggestions could spare further suffering and guide you to growth, should you choose the higher road of recovery:

1. **Don't deny**. No doubt, you'll want to wake from this reality. Some harmed are those closest, but many you will not know. You've confirmed their greatest fears that even family, friends, and leaders can stray from the paths they preach. None are immune to infidelity and that is earthshaking for most. Having broken the trust of the multitudes, know that your response to the wreckage speaks clearer to your attentive audience than any position you've proclaimed. Denial deepens distrust. Acceptance heightens *their* hopes and feeds *your* appetite for freedom.

2. **Take responsibility.** You were not a victim of your circumstances. Blaming your choices on couple conflict, a substandard sex life, or internal instability always proves pointless. Fixation on these factors can't contribute to change. You chose this path and can choose the next.

3. **Humbly seek specialized help.** Scanning the carnage of selfish choices stirs up self-hatred. Expect cravings that promise momentary escape from the stress of self-attack.[55] Resisting alone is a recipe for relapse. Humbly seek help that will hold you up. Certified specialists stand by, educated and equipped to pull you to safety. Since some doubters deny the science behind sexual addiction, seek *only* specialists. We won't downplay a sexual addiction's severity nor discount the trauma of those betrayed by your behavior. We will help you heal.

4. **Care for your wounded.** One word describes the impact of sexual betrayal on a partner: *trauma*. Your wife's world

has capsized and she is drenched in doubts. She wrestles with disappointment in the Divine. In this state of suffering, do not mistake her presence for allegiance. Should she stay or renounce the relationship, make her healing high priority. I have seen resilience after the devastation of disclosure. You both can learn to love. Also, don't let your children cascade through the cracks. They need to see a father who fights. I believe that will be you.

5. **Courageously hope.** Though the darkness is great, hope remains. Many before you have discovered life after the "wasted years"[56] more connected and meaningful than anything before. Such a recovery is possible yet hard-earned. Real recovery is a marathon, not a sprint.[57] This will be the most difficult goal you've pursued, requiring intense vulnerability and significant soul-digging. I believe you will transcend the apparent impossibility before you. With skilled support, you can find freedom, looking back on the day of your discovery as an unexpected, bittersweet blessing.

Mr. Duggar, as I see you caught by your consequences, I offer you compassion. This is not to condone your choices but because shame is never the catalyst for significant change.[58] The media will demonize you but I see a hurting human being.

You represent millions of men and women who are caught in addiction, tirelessly seeking to cope with their wounds and cover their tracks. My hope is that all who are secretly struggling will seek the support they so desperately require, not just for themselves but also for those who love them.

It takes courage to come out of hiding. But when we do, true healing can begin.[59]

Cheering you on,
Forest

CHAPTER 11

---◆———◆---

For the Christian Choosing Digital Adultery: Seven Strategies for Finding Freedom

---

Skill to Master #5: Learning to trust my Higher Power

Skill to Master #6: Protecting myself internally and externally

---

This piece was originally published in The Christian Leader magazine in 2016. While it is aimed at a Christian audience, sexual addicts from all spiritual backgrounds will benefit from the concepts presented herein.

Both God and pornography grabbed my attention at a young age. At age six, my father introduced me to Jesus and at twelve, a classmate presented me with pornography. For years these two loves would compete, as I sought to serve God while secretly hiding an insatiable hunger for self-destructive sexual indulgence. This conflict continued for over a decade. Years of false starts and self-induced suffering eventually resulted in surrender. I finally sought help.

How God redeemed my story is beyond belief. I am now a therapist who specializes in the treatment of sexual addiction. I teach and train therapists to assist individuals both overcome by addiction and overwhelmed by betrayal trauma. God continues to use my work and writing to bring hope and help to others.

Maybe you can relate to my story. The odds are that everyone reading this is either experiencing the draw of pornography or knows someone who is. Sadly, the Church is steeped in sexual addiction. Though too few are talking about it, many men, women, and children are mesmerized by this siren's song. Pornography has a strangle-hold on the Church, with an estimated 2/3 of Christian men and 1/3 of Christian women viewing it.[60] Adolescents between the ages of 12 to 17 are the largest consumers of pornography[61] and the estimated average age of first exposure is 11 years old.[62] In shame-driven isolation, too many stay silent.

Harmed Relationships

Pornography use harms all areas of life, especially relationships. Most couples come to me in crisis. So often, one partner experienced early exposure to pornography and believed the myth that married sex would substitute their sexual compulsivity. In shame, they concealed a secret addiction. This was the first betrayal that would someday surface. Maybe they abstained for a season but, eventually, when the stresses and struggles of life emerged, they often ran back to their comfort of choice: pornography.

When spouses seek a pixilated prostitute, they trade their relationship for wreckage. Here are three ways marriages are harmed when this happens:

1. **Hindering intimacy.** Connection and addiction cannot coexist in a relationship. [63] When one partner uses pornography addictively, it prevents intimacy. The connection that comes from reaching out to their spouse does not occur when they run to pornography to cope with life's pressures. Time and attention that could be invested in their relationship is instead spent on sexually compulsive pursuits.[64]

   A similar impact on one's relationship with God can also result. Repeatedly reaching to pornography rather than God's outstretched arms is the sad story of one who forsakes their "first love."[65] They must choose between lust and love but cannot have both.

2. **Stifling sexuality.** It is baffling to me that pornography is sometimes promoted as a sexual aid. If anything, pornography use diminishes sexual satisfaction. [66] Premature ejaculation[67] and erectile dysfunction[68] can be consequences. Not only can pornography use diminish sexual ability, it also alters sexual attitudes.[69] According to Covenant Eyes, 88 percent of porn scenes contain physical aggression and 49 percent contain verbal aggression.[70] It is no surprise that this skews views of sex. The "blessed" and satisfying sexuality hailed in Proverbs 5:18 is light-

years away from the demeaning distortion of sex
presented in most pornography.

3. **<u>Causing unparalleled pain.</u>** Even when sexual addiction
only involves pornography, it is often experienced as
infidelity. [71] Many partners who undergo this type of
relational trauma experience symptoms of PTSD, losing
their sense of safety. [72] These partners can experience
anxiety, depression, rage, hyper-vigilance, intrusive
thoughts, and shame. They may blame themselves,
becoming preoccupied with their body image. They may
lose trust in their spouse and in God. Sadly, these
symptoms often persist long after the day of discovery.
Covenant Eyes reported over half of divorce cases being
related to pornography addiction,[73] so it is apparent that
pornography use can poison a marriage.

Countless Consequences

Pornography use harms more than just marriages. Relationships
with children, God, and others are impacted. Neurologically,
self-control is impaired.[74] Self-image suffers. Witness to the world
is silenced. Justice is undermined, as the porn industry propels
sex trafficking forward.[75] No sphere of life is untouched. How
fitting that the plea of Proverbs is to keep to a path far from the
adulteress.[76]

Specific Strategies

For the reader who is ready to pursue a new path, here are
seven crucial strategies for finding freedom:

1. **Humble yourself.** Attitude is everything. Pride pours gas on the fires of addictive desires. Humility douses the flames. The sobering truth I see repeatedly is this: Find humility or humility will find you. The latter includes incomprehensible losses. Choose with great care.

2. **Find same-gender support.** Accountability is essential for both prevention and confession. When tempted, humbly call for help. Grace-based, not shame-based, support will sustain lasting change. Both addicts and partners can benefit from a guided group setting where their secrets are safe and their hearts can find healing.

3. **Go deep with God.** Brennan Manning writes that the journey from mistrust to trust can be like a "second conversion." [77] Letting God compassionately hold one's heart in trying and tempting times is much different than simply memorizing scripture. Both may be helpful but recovery will entail daily experiences *with* God, not just learning *about* God.

4. **External and internal protection.** Easy access to the portable prostitute is a trap. Protecting devices with filters and accountability software is often necessary. Implementing internal protection means learning self-care routines that strengthen self-control. Adequate sleep, exercise, and healthy eating will bolster the brain's resistance to temptation. [78] For those traumatized, self-care is equally essential.

5. **Seek out a skilled professional.** Stories abound of those who sought support in all the wrong places. Seeking someone who specializes in sexual addiction treatment can prevent unnecessary pain and promote lasting healing (See Week 1 of the *Recovery Roadmap*). This will be important for both addicts and their spouses. Couples in recovery must be coached as they learn how to connect, likely for the first time in the history of their marriage.

6. **Disclose with discretion.** Dumping every detail of a pornography problem on a partner can be detrimental. Honesty and transparency about the past and present are necessary but without the guidance of a trained professional, some specifics may cause unnecessary wounds.

7. **Be patient with your partner.** Recovery for both addicts and partners is a long-term commitment. Lasting change will require significant soul-work. Patience will provide endurance for the lengthy road ahead.

The Hope of Renewal

For both the reader who is far down the path of pornography and their traumatized spouse, there is hope. God has the unrivaled ability to resurrect that which was once dead. For those who have humbly sought help, I have seen relationships reconditioned to a new level of intimacy. There may be years between the present reality and a healed marriage. Yet, this rough road to recovery is far superior to the instability of a divided heart, the despair of disconnection, and the anguish of an unfulfilled life lost to lust.

I believe God is raising up a Church that rejects pornography and seeks authentic connection. As God unshackles us, He invites us into His mission of setting captives free. Though this path to healing is steep and treacherous at times, it is incredibly rewarding. And the view from the top is spectacular. It is my steadfast hope that someday I'll see you there.

CHAPTER 12

Disclosure 101:
The Art of Coming Clean

---

*Skill to Master #7: Disclosing to my partner my acting out history
with the help of a trained professional*

Secrets are the driving force of sexual addiction.[79] When secrets are maintained, sexual addiction is sustained. When sexual addicts strive to hide their compulsive coping, it leads to double-lives shrouded by lies. When this deception is discovered, relationships are devastated. A partner in this situation is very vulnerable. Not knowing what to do, they may demand details, grasping for some sense of certainty. Overwhelmed with shame, the addict may remain speechless or reactively say too much. Sadly, if the addict's secrets are not disclosed with discretion, serious consequences can ensue. This dynamic can be the death of relationships.

Thankfully, there is an alternative. With the right help, couples caught in these circumstances can do a facilitated Disclosure. What is a Disclosure? Sexual addiction therapist Alexandra Katehakis defines Disclosure as "a structured confession wherein the addict takes full responsibility for everything that he or she has done in the way of acting out sexually."[80] In a Disclosure, the sexual addict is carefully guided through the process of writing out their acting out history then methodically presenting it to their partner.

The prospect of coming clean through this kind of confession can be terrifying for a sexual addict. It is common to question this process. Disclosure done right can be powerful for both partners but before they begin, they should know the purposes of undertaking this endeavor. Understanding why Disclosure can be so meaningful can increase the addict's motivation to proceed with this bold venture.

A while back, I did a SATP interview with LifeSTAR therapist Geoff Steurer, LMFT, an expert and author in the area of sexual addiction Disclosure. [81] For those courageously considering doing a Disclosure, think about these seven purposes that Geoff shared with me that day:

1. **To bring the couple into reality.** Geoff started by quoting the Russian proverb, "Better to be slapped with the truth than kissed with a lie." Disclosure is an opportunity to bring a much-needed reality to the relationship. Disclosure sheds light on unanswered questions, helping the couple see the situation for what it really is.

2. **To aid the addict in facing themselves.** If a sexual addict fails to face themselves, they will continue living the lies. The false life they've created is the path to perpetual pain that the addict will want to numb out by returning to addictive behaviors. When the addict faces their partner, and tells the truth, they face themselves. Facing themselves in the Disclosure, the addict experiences healing as they own and settle into their story of sex addiction.

3. **To reduce the addict's shame.** In Disclosure, the addict comes out of hiding. When the addict is finally fully seen, shame decreases.

4. **To clarify future decisions.** Only when the truth is disclosed, can the couple make accurate decisions about the future. When the addict sees themselves clearly, they can decide what they want to do, rather than continually deceiving themselves. In the light of the truth, the partner can also make informed decisions about their future, whether they remain in the relationship or decide to move on. In Disclosure, the partner is provided the decency to decide what's next after finally looking at all the pieces of the story. If the partner chose to stay in their relationship prior to the Disclosure, they really weren't choosing the relationship, because they were basing their choice on an incomplete, inaccurate perspective. Without the Disclosure, the addict in secret-keeping mode will live with the lingering insecurity, doubting whether their partner wants to be with them or not. In this state, the fear and shame remain. In Disclosure, the addict tells

their partner all they have done. If a partner chooses to stay after hearing everything, the addict won't doubt the motivations driving their decision. The fear and shame are stripped away from their relational bond.

5. **To reverse the order of information.** A partner may believe that discovery and interrogation are the only strategies to learn the truth, a perspective based on personal experience. In Disclosure, the burden to bring complete and accurate information falls fully on the addict. This sets a powerful precedent. For the first time, the partner won't have to wrestle to conjure up the right questions. In Disclosure, they hear the truth flowing in a new direction: from the addict to the partner. This is a critical step toward rebuilding trust.

6. **To reveal true remorse.** When the addict shares their secrets from a reactive stance, the partner won't recognize the addict's remorse. When the delivery of very sensitive information sounds something like, "Fine! Here's everything!" the addict's tone of regret is absent. In a reactive state, the addict is in fight-or-flight, unable to connect with the softer part of their heart. But in Disclosure, the partner has a new experience. The partner can sense the addict is sincerely sorry, seeing the softening in their face and eyes. What the partner witnesses and feels as they experience the Disclosure is something that could never come from late night discoveries, interrogations, or yelling matches. This moves the partner toward the possibility of forgiveness.

7. **To bring wholeness.** The Disclosure helps the addict become whole and the couple become *one*. When the couple is one, they see the same story. Divisions and barriers are brought down. Nothing facilitates oneness quite like the process of Disclosure.

Geoff described Disclosure as an early, necessary stage of recovery, where the addict is freed from the need to manage their secrets. Disclosure can produce deep pain for the partner but, as Geoff pointed out, it is lesser than the pain of being lied to long-term. Packaged with the pain, partners often experience relief. Following Disclosure, the secrets that haunted both partners are no longer hidden in darkness.

The Potential Damage of Do-It-Yourself Disclosures
While Disclosures can play a substantial role in a couple's recovery, a Disclosure done haphazardly can have devastating results. That's one reason why attempting an at-home Disclosure is such a bad idea. Dumping traumatizing information on the partner outside the structure provided by a professional is negligence, plain and simple. A do-it-yourself Disclosure could result in damage when essential information is omitted, the wrong details are described, a prideful attitude is present, no support system is in place, the addict places blame on the partner, or countless other dynamics are present. The lesson should be obvious: Don't try this at home.

My strong suggestion for sexual addicts considering Disclosure is that they seek out a sexual addiction therapist who has been trained to do Disclosures and has practice facilitating them. They can help couples navigate the need for any immediate disclosure due to potential risk factors (like STI's) and facilitate a successful execution of the Disclosure experience that minimizes the damage. The therapist can also explore with a couple the possibility of disclosing to other family members (like adolescent or adult children), if needed. A sexual addiction therapist can help a couple set up a system for disclosing future acting out or lying incidences if they occur, helping them prevent new secrets from taking root.

For those planning to bypass the Disclosure process out of fear, consider Geoff's words of warning:

Regardless if the behavior is pornography, sexual acting out with another person, or anything else, it's critical that the injured partner know the reality of the situation. Failure to disclose is essentially stealing someone else's reality from them.[82]

That being said, there is the possibility a professional may caution against proceeding with a Disclosure for various reasons. At least the addict in this case has thoughtfully considered their options, allowing someone who is trained to assess their situation and make informed recommendations.

A Disclosure session is the most carefully planned session I facilitate with my clients. I follow a specific process of preparation and execution that proves successful. Disclosures are by far one of the bravest and hardest steps a couple can take on their pathway to healing. But many have discovered that this honest endeavor is an investment in long-term freedom from secrets that once fueled their addiction and were the source of their partner's greatest pain. When the truth is finally known, the truth sets couples free.[83]

CHAPTER 13

The Paradox of Pornography Addiction: What You Fear Most Will Heal You[84]

Skill to Master #8*: Learning to connect in the context of a recovery group*

What if the one thing you feared most was the source of your deepest healing? This is the paradox of pornography addiction. In shame, porn addicts seek safety in the shadows of isolation. The sad irony is that in doing so, they separate themselves from a profound source of healing: authentic and accepting relationships.

After years of pursuing personal recovery and helping others heal as well, I am convinced that learning to connect with others in a group setting is foundational for long-term recovery. Without the group experience, recovery attempts are destined to fail.

For most, participation in a group sounds scary. Porn addicts tend to have a strong aversion to the concept, even when told that groups are vital. Let me explain why porn addicts are repelled by the idea of recovery groups.

Most of us who struggle with pornography addiction learned early in life that other people could not be trusted to meet our needs. Whether this lesson came through neglect, abuse, or trauma, this belief made us vulnerable to porn addiction.[85] When denied the connection we were wired for, we started looking for alternative connections.

In times of stress or distress, all humans reach out for soothing. Since our track record with people was poor, we turned to something non-relational to escape our suffering.[86] For us, pornography quickly became the source of all soothing. At first, it seemed to meet a need but eventually we were overwhelmed by an out-of-control addiction. What was meant to be our solution became our new source of suffering.[87]

With this all too common backstory, our greatest need in recovery is the connection that seems to eternally evade us. As Carl Jung once said, "We are wounded in relationship and we heal through relationship."[88]

Here are three powerful reasons why groups provide the connection necessary for a lifetime of healing, even though the idea of opening up may be what is most feared:

1. **We learn to trust.** Though we have been hurt by others in our past, groups provide a safe context in which we can learn to trust again. It is in groups that we get to practice

connecting with others, possibly for the first time in our life. As we trust the group more fully, we open up more fully. The miracle of recovery occurs when love begins to fill us in a way that lust never could. This transformative experience cannot occur in isolation, so groups are essential.

2. **<u>Our shame and secrecy diminish.</u>** Nothing fuels addiction like secrecy and shame. Active in our addiction, we believe we are innately broken and unworthy of love. Unless we learn to give voice to our inadequacies and hidden transgressions amongst those who support us, our addiction will thrive. Groups provide a safe and confidential setting where we can share our shame-saturated secrets. As frightening as it may be initially, when we allow safe people to see inside of us, our shame is stunted and we develop a sense of belonging. While we once lived shackled by secrets, we experience how living in the truth sets us free.

3. **<u>We find strength in numbers.</u>** When we join a group, we suddenly have a team working for the good of each player. We are stronger together. Groups provide both a cheering section and a lifeline. In times of temptation, there is power in reaching out to fellow group members. I liken this experience to letting someone talk us back from a dangerous ledge. In my personal battle against sexual addiction, having a handful of caring friends that I can call or text in moments of weakness or pain has strengthened my recovery in unimaginable ways.

Replacing Lust with Love.

I am both a group leader and a group member. These days I lead eight recovery groups and participate in two recovery groups per week. Having helped many porn addicts find freedom, I can honestly say that without a group, real recovery is impossible. Sure, someone might achieve *sobriety* on their own. But in order to recover from an often debilitating and lifelong addiction, a person needs to do more than just let go of lust.

As I shared in a workbook I wrote for my clients, "recovery is a process of letting go of lust and letting love replace it. It means letting go of your attachment to unhealthy coping mechanisms and connecting with what is real. Learning how to connect will likely be the hardest yet most rewarding adventure of your life. Connection truly satisfies what lust never could."[89]

It is my hope that those seeking long-term freedom from pornography addiction will lean into the fear of being seen and take the bold leap of joining a recovery group.

When we come out of hiding, healing can begin.

CHAPTER 14

Five Reasons to Fire Your
Accountability Partner[90]

---

*Skill to Master #9: Learning to connect through a same-gender
accountability relationship*

If you're like most sex addicts, you prefer porn over people.
Looking back through your personal history you may recall
an extensive track record of running to your pixilated
prostitutes. It was always there when you thought you needed a
quick fix. But people are less predictable and trusting others
often feels both unnatural and unnecessary. Yet, when porn
addicts finally decide to seriously seek recovery, they quickly
learn that finding an accountability partner is an essential
element of lasting change. Pushing past their initial resistance,

those who bravely seek connection through an accountability relationship are on the road to real recovery.

But sometimes the partners we pick are far from a good fit for us. I'm not just pointing to personality conflicts here. We are all imperfect human beings who will have imperfect relationships. But sometimes it becomes clear that firing an accountability partner is the wisest thing we can do.

Whether you are questioning the fit of a current accountability partner or just looking to learn how to find (or improve) an accountability-based relationship, consider these five *red flags* that may mean some significant changes are necessary for the best growth to occur.

1. **<u>A lukewarm attitude.</u>** If your accountability partner downplays the seriousness of lust, porn, or sex addiction, this is a problem. You might hear them use minimizing phrases like "everyone does it" or "you can look but you can't touch." Maybe it becomes clear that your partner is uncommitted to their own battle against lust. With a watered-down commitment, how can they be a source of strength to you? Sure, there are short seasons when motivation slumps but long-term complacency is a recipe for relapse. In recovery, it is essential that your partner takes sex addiction seriously. When they don't, their role as an accountability partner is compromised.

2. **<u>Unavailability.</u>** When your partner is too busy to respond, they cannot rightly fulfill their role. Learning to reach out in times of temptation and distress is essential in recovery. In order to do this, you need an accountability partner who is available, both physically and emotionally. This

does not mean your partner's life must revolve around yours. But it does mean that they take some time to talk on the phone or meet in person. If they can't listen in a moment of need, they can call you back later (which is why having a list of people to call is recommended). But divisive resentment can quickly arise when your partner is unwilling to invest the minimal time it takes to support you in your recovery. How can you learn to trust others and connect without experiencing another's faithful, caring response? A partner's excessive busyness can be a sign that the accountability relationship is going south.

3. **Fear of confrontation.** Most people are afraid of "rocking the boat" but when your accountability partner won't question and challenge you, they do you a disservice. As you proceed forward in your recovery, you'll need someone with the courage to ask the hard questions. If your partner sees you slipping in your commitments, moving into tempting situations, or stepping toward addiction in any way, you need them to alert you of the looming disaster. Part of your partner's role is to shine light on your blind spots and remind you of your commitments. If you notice them avoiding the hard conversations, repeatedly trying to please you, and side-stepping all conflict, there is cause to be wary about their fit as your accountability partner.

4. **Shaming.** If your partner shames or demeans you, this will hurt, not help, you. If the main person you confess your wrongs and weaknesses to has a tendency to metaphorically bash you over the head every time you

relapse or make a mistake, not only will you avoid those hard conversations but you will also be less likely to change. Certainly, guilt is good because it can motivate change when you see the impact of your destructive behavior. But when shamed, you will feel like you are the problem, not your choices. While many of us think that self-hate will motivate us, the truth is it does just the opposite; it disempowers us.[91] So, if you walk away from time with your partner constantly feeling demoralized, take this as a significant sign that something needs to change.

5. **<u>Lack of love.</u>** If your accountability partner cares about your behavior but discounts your suffering, the trust that breeds change will never sprout and grow. Many sexual addicts grew up in environments where their feelings were ignored or punished, driving them, in a sense, toward non-relational comforts like pornography and compulsive masturbation.[92] In recovery, letting go of false and fantasy comforts will only work for the long-term when replaced with real connections. If you sense that when you share your buried and resurrected feelings and secrets with your partner they fall on deaf ears, this will remind you why you stopped trusting in the first place and make pornography appear all the more alluring. You will want to numb out and escape your uncared for feelings. So, if your partner tells you to "suck it up" and is unwilling to learn how to sit with you in your pain, it may be time to part ways.

If any of these five warning signs describe your accountability partner, don't just drop them immediately. First, do the more difficult thing; go to them and address these issues. Then, if they are unwilling to change or grow in these areas, you have permission to fire them. If you do decide it is time to part ways, do so with care. Don't create an enemy by how you end. Thank them for their initial willingness and for their efforts. Commit to keep all of your conversations confidential. Wish them well, then promptly begin your search for a replacement. You can use these guidelines as a roadmap to finding a more fitting recovery partner.

I have discovered in my own recovery that having an accountability partner that takes my struggles seriously, invests time and attention, speaks the truth in love,[93] strengthens me without shaming me, and cares for my past and current wounds is both transformational and life-giving. He is not my first accountability partner but eventually our paths were meant to cross and I am grateful.

May you seek and find the right fit too.

CHAPTER 15

———◆——————◆———

The Neuroscience of Self-Care[94]

Skill to Master #10: Consistent and effective self-care

"What's the one piece of advice you would give to someone struggling with porn addiction?" This was the question posed by Stephen Kuhn, author of *10 Lies Men Believe About Porn,* in our online interview.[95]

My answer may surprise you.

I focused on the neuroscience of self-care because it is an essential, yet easily overlooked, component of a successful recovery plan. In recovery myself, I know all too well that when we don't invest time in self-care, we will waste time in addiction. As I shared in the interview, "When I think of recovery, I think of it as a lifestyle change, wherein we're moving from a lifestyle of self-neglect and self-destructive behavior to a lifestyle of self-care."

In my view, without consistent self-care, there is no long-term recovery. We may abstain for a period of time but eventually stress and other triggers will catch up with us. Once we understand how self-care impacts us neurologically, self-care becomes a *no-brainer* for those in recovery.

Sexual addiction impairs the pre-frontal cortex of the brain.[96] One of the necessary functions of the pre-frontal cortex is providing self-control. According to neurosurgeon Dr. Donald Hilton, impairment of the pre-frontal cortex leads to many problems, including impulsivity, compulsivity, and impaired judgment.[97] The more a person acts out sexually, the less self-control they will have to stop themselves from acting on future impulses. This is a vicious cycle. It explains why both abstinence and the practice of brain strengthening activities are an essential part of the recovery process. What follows are some specific self-care strategies that strengthen the brain, thus strengthening recovery.

The Necessity of Sleep: Strengthening the Brain to Resist Relapse

One night as I sat comfortably on my couch watching an informational video on my laptop, my experience was abruptly interrupted by my computer's loss of power. I shrugged it off as an excuse to go to bed. In the morning I was surprised to find my computer cord on the floor, within arms' reach from where I sat the previous evening. My power supply was with me the whole time, yet I failed to reach out for it.

What a perfect picture of how many of us move through life. We crawl through our days feeling as though we're running on fumes, while one of our most powerful sources of strength is within our reach. This simple practice that exponentially improves our lives in both quality and length and without which we experience unprecedented suffering is something all humans require - sleep!

Sleep is a necessity for everyone, especially those recovering from addiction. In fact, successful recovery and practicing healthy sleep habits are inseparable. Lack of sufficient sleep is a primary trigger for many. When I am sleep-deprived, my Evil Genius shows up. My mindset shifts from what I am fighting for to what I can get away with. In that state of mind, I can't trust myself. I creatively pursue self-destruction rather than my recovery commitments. I am in dangerous territory. If I don't prioritize catching up on sleep immediately, I will likely make decisions that increase my tiredness and remorse.

It turns out that sleep has a potent effect on the addicted brain, proving to be one of the most influential factors in successful recovery. In *The Brain Fix*, Dr. Ralph Carson describes why recovering addicts require adequate sleep.[98] He explains how the high demands of treatment, such as being ready to learn and accepting a new way of living, cannot be embraced with the right attitude without the foundation of quality sleep. When recovering addicts fail to "wake up feeling refreshed, responsive, positive, and committed to the hard work of recovery," their treatment progress is compromised.[99] Sleep also provides the brain the opportunity to organize information that it has learned.[100]

Of special interest to those in recovery, sleep impacts the pre-frontal cortex of the brain. In her talk at Google,[101] Dr. Kelly McGonigal, Stanford psychology professor and author of *The Willpower Instinct*, explained how sleep deprivation affects the brain, showing images of its impact. She described how sleep deprivation inhibits the pre-frontal cortex's ability to work efficiently, making it more difficult to remember important goals. She shared about a study where addicts increased the duration of their sleep, experiencing a strengthened ability to resist addictive cravings. Basically, being sleep-starved diminishes self-control but being well-rested increases it. This is incredibly significant for sex addicts who are working hard to achieve sobriety and build new recovery habits.

Dr. Ralph Carson echoes this research, writing about additional impacts of having a pre-frontal cortex that is "shut down" due to poor sleep. He explains how this state of mind can lead to overreaction to difficult situations, moodiness, impatience, and overall irritability.[102] For those in recovery, these negative mood states can be extremely triggering, increasing the temptation to relapse.

Take some time and think about your personal sleep habits. Maybe you have a job that interferes with a consistent sleep schedule. Maybe you're a parent of little ones who are less able to achieve a full night's rest. Maybe you have difficulty unwinding at night so you stay up late hoping to de-stress. Maybe your eating or drinking habits impede your ability to fall asleep quickly. Maybe there is a medical or psychological reason why deep sleep is hard to come by. If you relate to any of these scenarios, I urge you to consider your options. You may need to ask for help. You may need to restructure your life in significant ways. For those who do not make necessary changes to improve sleep, this will contribute to difficulty remaining sober and self-controlled.

Sleep deprivation clearly affects us mentally, physically, emotionally, relationally, and neurologically. For those facing challenges requiring sustained self-control, sleep is essential. Thus, implementing consistent, quality sleep practices proves to be a necessary component of a successful recovery plan. I urge you to consider the results of good rest and make the changes that will improve your life in countless ways.

Exercise: Good for the Body, Great for the Brain

We are all looking for that miracle experience that will infuse us with the power to reach our goals. For those striving to attain seemingly impossible achievements, such as recovering from an addiction, finding strength boosters will be an essential part of the journey. Exercise is another empowering recovery habit, with multiple benefits.

In Dr. Kelly McGonigal's video entitled *Brain Science: A Miracle Cure For Willpower*, she describes exercise as a "willpower miracle," based on the current science.[103] Exercise is another practice that strengthens the pre-frontal cortex, increasing self-control.

Exercise strengthens recovery also because of its mood-boosting benefits. Emotional states such as depression and anxiety can be especially triggering for sexual addicts. ADHD is a common disorder amongst sexual addicts as well.[104] Exercise is helpful with all of these mental illness challenges.[105] Professional help is also recommended. When we are managing our moods well, we are less triggered to seek out ways to escape them.

Another way that exercise strengthens recovery is through its impact on resilience. In his book *Spark: The Revolutionary New Science of Exercise and the Brain*, Dr. John Ratey shares that increased fitness corresponds with increased resilience.[106] Due to the difficulty of addiction recovery, resilience is a valuable commodity. This is going to be very hard. It will require consistency and perseverance.

There are countless other benefits of exercise for those in recovery (See the *Addiction* chapter in *Spark* for additional information). I agree with Dr. Ratey's assertion that addicts should maintain a habit of consistent exercise.[107] Exercise, he says, is an effective means of "rewiring the brain to circumvent the addictive pattern and curbing the craving."[108] The regular practice of this powerful tool leads to increased internal strength in difficult moments, laying the foundation for a lifetime of meaningful changes.

The Scary Side of Sugar: The Trick of Treats

Halloween is a celebration of sugar. Cloaked in creative costumes, we savor sweets in several settings, whether parading from house to house with kiddos or partying with friends. Somehow these evenings often end with a massive sugar stash or a major sugar crash. They are often inseparable. But for those in recovery, is there a hidden danger in this excessive consumption of sugar? Is it wise for addicts in recovery to limit their consumption of sweets or is sugar intake irrelevant? I have wondered this for some time myself.

In an article by Christina Veselak, LMFT, *Relapse and Sugar Dysregulation*, these questions are addressed head on. Veselak explains that "consuming a high sugar diet" is a "primary relapse trigger for all recovering addicts."[109] As it turns out, eating simple carbohydrates (like candy) has a rapid effect on blood sugar that can be detrimental to those in recovery. Her article describes why this is true, noting how blood sugar spikes can disrupt the addict's mood, which can be triggering. Conversely, when blood sugar drops, addictive cravings can increase. Dr.

Kelly McGonigal echoes this perspective, sharing how these blood sugar peaks and valleys negatively impact the brain.[110] In her book *The Willpower Instinct*, she describes how excessive sugar obliterates self-control. For these reasons, it appears evident that eating excessive sugar can be a strong trigger for addictive behavior.

Another harmful character trait of sugar is that it is highly addictive. In times of stress or suffering, choosing not to turn to one's drug of choice but instead to sugar can create a new dependency. Since sexual addiction and sugar both provide a quick dopamine fix, it is no surprise that sugar can be sought out when an addict is trying to stay sexually sober. This is not successful recovery but instead trading one addiction for another.

Sex addiction therapist Robert Weiss writes about the potential for cross-addiction, sharing a scenario where one woman worked a seemingly successful recovery program for one addiction, yet packed on dozens of pounds in her first year of sobriety.[111] I have observed that sugar, and food in general, is often the recovering sex addict's second choice for comfort as they pursue sexual sobriety. This is one reason why "addictions, not just the primary addiction but any secondary addictions, must be addressed head-on, often simultaneously, because if the addict doesn't heal from all of the problems, he or she might not heal from any." [112]

In light of this information, what can be done? Dr. McGonigal recommends avoiding blood sugar crashes by eating foods that give you lasting energy.[113] Similarly, in *The Physiology of Willpower: Linking Blood Glucose to Self-Control*, Matthew Gailliot explains that "restoring glucose to a sufficient level typically improves self-control." [114] Healthy eating in recovery is also important because the brain that is healing from addiction requires specific nutrients to rebuild itself.[115]

With this information as a guide, it is recommended that moderation and mindfulness be exercised on both sugar-saturated holidays and in everyday life. It is my hope that this information will not limit your enjoyment of the festivities but instead add to a more meaningful experience with minimal triggers.

The Mindful Breathing Boost

Another self-care practice that strengthens recovery is mindful breathing. I recommend this to clients struggling with impulsivity, whether it manifests in addiction or out of control anger. Curt Thompson, MD, explains the process of neuroplasticity, sharing that "If I want my brain to change, I need to change the focus of my attention."[116] One method of doing this is an exercise he calls a *Six Breaths Per Minute Exercise*, that can be done daily. This intentional, focused way of breathing strengthens self-control. Dr. Kelly McGonigal writes about a similar version where someone focuses on the feeling of the breath and redirecting the mind back to the breath every time it wanders away. [117] This exercise is one of many mindfulness practices that increase willpower.[118]

The Power of Practice

As we consider all of the ways self-care shapes our brains, it is evident that it plays a significant role in recovery work. While this may sound simple, it is not easy. To create the healthy lifestyle that will empower your recovery, I highly recommend the implementation of rituals. In their relevant book *The Power of Full Engagement,* Loehr and Schwartz share that "All great performers rely on positive rituals to manage their energy and regulate their behavior."[119] If we want our self-care practices to transition from being a burden into being our auto-pilot, ritualized habits will lead us there.

I have found that starting the day with scheduled self-care rituals gives me the most momentum. Rising out of bed at 6am after a good eight hours of sleep, going for a 20-minute run while listening to inspiring music or talks, enjoying 20 minutes of prayer/journaling/quiet time in the early morning air as the sun rises, then doing five to ten minutes of focused breathing followed by five minutes of recovery reading - to me, this is an ideal morning ritual that automatizes many of the recovery habits I want to practice the rest of my life. It is a rewarding feeling when I've started my day right.

Many people will need help planning and executing healthy practices, at least in the beginning. This is one benefit of participating in a structured sexual addiction treatment program. Also, it is recommended that those wishing to change their self-care habits consult a doctor as needed.

For those in recovery, learning to care for self is a momentous undertaking. For addicts, self-care can feel awkward and undeserved. Self-care may seem selfish but it is not. When we learn to master self-care, we have the greatest shot at recovery from a life of self-neglect and addiction. This undertaking is unbelievably hard but worth all the effort when we reap the quality of life that results.

CHAPTER 16

Permission to Rest[120]

Skill to Master #11*: *Healthy self-soothing and relaxation

As a person in recovery, I find it consistently challenging to give myself the rest and relaxation I need. What comes naturally for me is overcommitment and overachievement. I can easily prioritize productivity over caring for myself responsibly. Too often, guilt goes hand-in-hand with giving myself a break. I know I am not alone in this. Flores writes that addicts "demonstrate an almost complete inability to relax and enjoy themselves."[121] Learning the lifestyle of effective self-care takes continuous effort. For me, it is a journey of constant course correction.

Thankfully, my body tells me when I am maxing out my resources and my capacity for productivity. I have learned to see addictive cravings as signals that something is not right inside of me. When those signals go off, it is time to act (prevention is even better). If I do not respond with attention, curiosity, and care, I know I am on the road to relapse.

In her book *Running On Empty*, Dr. Jonice Webb shares that "adults who were emotionally neglected as children often don't know what their needs are. Their own wants, needs, and feelings are not only irrelevant to the emotionally neglected, they're invisible." [122] Since many sexual addicts were emotionally neglected in early life, [123] it makes sense where we learned to neglect ourselves.

Dr. Webb recommends finding "healthy self-soothing strategies" that fit each individual's needs. [124] They could range from going for a walk in the woods, praying or meditating, listening to peaceful music, writing or journaling, exercising, playing with a pet, taking a bath, reading in a hammock, or gardening. The possibilities are endless. We can discover and regularly practice the healthy, non-addictive activities that meet our deepest needs.

We can learn how to love ourselves in many ways, as part of our daily rituals and in times of heightened stress. We benefit from a weekly day of rest and time off throughout our year to recuperate and reconnect. We can continually seek the support we need and remind ourselves that today is a great day to begin again. This self-compassionate and self-supportive approach will help us get off of the hamster-wheel of performance and pay attention to the things that are most needed. In many ways, we are becoming our own loving parent, learning to care for ourselves in a protective yet nurturing manner. [125]

For those of us who cannot shake the misinformed notion that rest is not productive, the opposite is true. It turns out that intentionally alternating between activity and rest is a strategy for heightening performance.[126] At key times, rest can be the most productive thing we can do. When we learn to rest really well, we rejuvenate and ready ourselves to re-engage in productive, focused, and meaningful work.

May we all learn to tune in to the needs of our body, mind, and soul, investing in the much needed care that will soothe our wounds and wholly revitalize us.

Let's officially give ourselves permission to rest.

CHAPTER 17

—◆——————◆—

Dealing with "Demons":
Healing from a Shame-Based
Identity[127]

Skill to Master #12: Shame management

D o you ever feel like there is a horrific beast inside of you?
Have you thought that something is deeply wrong inside,
experiencing disconnection from those around you?

Do you maintain a beautiful exterior life while "demons" of
shame haunt you internally?

If so, then you've experienced something commonplace for
sexual addicts. The sexual addict's shame can be the result of
serious trauma, abuse, and/or self-destructive choices. Much like
the *Demons* music video by Imagine Dragons, someone saturated

in shame can fit in with the crowd while deeply suffering internally. In recovery, the sexual addict must understand shame and learn how to manage it well for lasting healing to occur.

What is Shame?

Shame is much different than guilt. Shame researcher Brené Brown explains that guilt says "I did something bad" whereas shame says "I am bad."[128] Those who live with this shame-based mentality tend to view their addictive choices as proof that they're terrible people rather than seeing mistakes as opportunities to learn and grow.

Carl Jung said that "Shame is a soul eating emotion."[129] When it feels like hell inside, it's no wonder sexual addicts want to escape to something comforting and familiar. Despite its destructive nature, addiction feels safe, especially when early traumatic events teach addicts that people are unsafe. For sexual addicts, this belief plays a key role in their intimacy disorder.[130]

Feeling broken and unlovable, sexual addicts often assume others will reject them. Patrick Carnes describes this dynamic writing that "fear of abandonment and shame are at the core of addiction."[131] Sadly, sexual addicts shelter themselves from others, keeping relationships at an arm's distance. Brené Brown describes shame's power in this way:

Shame is the intensely painful feeling or experience of believing that we are flawed and therefore unworthy of love and belonging. It's the fear that something we've done or failed to do, an ideal that we've not lived up to, or a goal that we've not accomplished makes us unworthy of connection. I'm not worthy or good enough for love, belonging, or connection. I'm unlovable. I don't belong.[132]

Maintaining this mindset that they are uniquely flawed, isolation and withdrawal become a way of life for sexual addicts. Addiction is often rooted in this shame-based identity.[133] The shame remains, like a low-grade fever, and it doesn't dissipate on its own. That is one reason why long-term recovery means more than just abstaining from addictive behavior.[134] Healing the roots of addiction requires the harder work of healing from a shame-based identity.

The Way of Escape

Despite feelings to the contrary, there is a route of escape for those battling internal "demons" of shame. The most powerful antidote to shame I've discovered is authentic connection. This comes in the forms of self-connection through self-compassion and connection to others through vulnerability, honesty, and experiencing empathy.[135]

Inward Connection

Self-compassion is foreign to those suffering from deep shame. But, when practiced over time, it can become an avenue of powerful healing. Self-compassion is a useful practice that supports recovery from addiction,[136] trauma, and a shame-based identity.[137] It is an effective tool for decreasing self-criticism,[138] managing emotional pain,[139] and promoting positive change.[140] Learning to respond to feelings and needs in a self-compassionate manner facilitates deeper connection with self, supporting long-term healing. Self-compassion not only decreases shame but may also alleviate anxiety, depression, feelings of inferiority, and self-attacks.[141]

Beverly Engel explains that when a shameful memory is wired into the brain, it can be repaired through self-compassion and self-empathy.[142] Mastering the art of self-compassion is a key component of successful recovery. Dr. Kristen Neff provides a plethora of self-compassion resources through her website, book, and workshops.

Outward Connection

Letting safe people see into the dark places within can be an incredibly frightening yet healing experience. In her book *Daring Greatly*, Brené Brown shares that "shame derives its power from being unspeakable...If we cultivate enough awareness about shame to name it and speak to it, we've basically cut it off at the knees. Shame hates having words wrapped around it. If we speak shame, it begins to whither."

Learning to be vulnerable, to trust others, to reach out in times of distress and pain, and to share experiences that are related to past and present shame, all play a part in recovering from a shame-based identity. Therapy groups and recovery groups are a great place to begin this process of healing. Individual therapy can provide necessary connection and healing as well, especially for those experiencing the effects of trauma and abuse. Learning to connect to self, to others, and to a Higher Power will also contribute to healing from a shame-based identity.

May those who battle destructive demons find light in the eyes of those who have been there yet live unbound by the shackles of shame. May this road of authentic connection lead to a life of motivating hope, joyous freedom, and heart-felt healing.

CHAPTER 18

—◆———◆—

The Courage of Self-Connection[143]

Skill to Master #13: *Self-connection*

Skill to Master #14: *Self-compassion*

Skill to Master #15: *Emotional regulation (managing pain and emotion)*

Something is under the surface, can you feel it? You've sensed it many times, yet still don't know what it is. You keep moving forward, keep staying busy, keep ignoring it, keep pretending everything's fine. But it's not. Something is unsettled inside but you're too busy to feel it. It's moments like this when addiction whispers messages like "escape there" and "run here."

And all of this is for what purpose? To keep running, keep escaping, keep distracting? This is the cycle of disconnection from self. For some, this pattern was learned at a very young age. For many, this pattern is instinctual.

Stopping and turning toward yourself, connecting with what is inside, and being kind toward whatever is hiding in the shadows of your soul requires great courage. This is scary, uncharted territory. Yet, for those who never take this risk, distraction becomes their drug of choice. Self-neglect and self-abandonment continue as the self-defeating norms.

Yet some of the most profound moments in life will be those times when you stop, see your pain, feel the surfacing emotions, and respond with care, compassion, and nurturance. This is tending to your wounds. This is attuning to the cries of your heart. Learning to effectively regulate emotion is foundational for those seeking recovery from sexual addiction.

If you have never learned how to relate to yourself like this, consider beginning today. Instead of grabbing the laptop, the bottle, the drug, or the sugar, consider grabbing a pen and connecting with the emotions you are running from. This can be done through journaling your feelings but the most powerful form of self-connection I've discovered is practicing self-compassion.

Mastering self-compassion tools will help you stop the cycle of disconnection in its tracks. It helps you learn to connect and find the comfort you've always needed. This will be worth the time and effort. It is a monumental step on the path of recovery.

Why Self-Compassion?

Self-compassion is a powerful tool for recovering addicts, with multiple benefits. Over a hundred journal articles point to conclusive results that self-compassion is "predictive of psychological well-being"[144] in many areas. Dr. Kristen Neff has researched self-compassion for many years and reports that "people who are compassionate to themselves are much less likely to be depressed, anxious, and stressed, and are much more likely to be happy, resilient, and optimistic about their future. In short, they have better mental health."[145]

You may be wondering, "What is self-compassion?" Dr. Kelly McGonigal describes self-compassion as "being kind and supportive to yourself whenever you experience suffering."[146] It means learning to show yourself care and concern in the same way that you would with someone you love who is going through a difficult experience, whether it is the result of personal choices or challenging life circumstances.

The abilities to connect with self and manage emotional states are foundational to long-term recovery. In the book *Addiction as an Attachment Disorder,* Flores writes that "until addicts develop the capacity to use their feelings as signals and to become emotionally intimate with themselves, they will continue to engage in their self-destructive and self-defeating behavior."[147] Self-compassion is a useful vehicle to deepen this kind of self-connection, with life-changing implications.

Learning how to find healthy comfort when experiencing distress or suffering is a key recovery skill. Many people in recovery experience intense levels of shame and are self-critical with themselves as a result. Self-criticism produces cortisol[148] and inhibits change. [149] Interestingly, self-compassion decreases cortisol and produces oxytocin,[150] which decreases cravings[151] and leads to feelings of calm and safety. [152] The "feelings of warmth, safety, presence, and interconnectedness" produced through self-compassion "alleviate emotion dysregulation," [153] providing significant help to suffering addicts.

There are many exercises that help people begin to relate to themselves with self-compassion. One of the most potent self-compassion exercises available is called the *Self-Compassion Break* (one version of this exercise is presented in the next chapter). It offers a quick opportunity to implement the three components of self-compassion: mindfulness, common humanity, and self-kindness.[154]

The Self-Compassion Break is so simple that it may easily be minimized or disregarded. However, when used in moments of pain or suffering, this exercise proves to be one of the most effective tools we have at our disposal for regulating emotion, connecting with self, and experiencing comfort in difficult times. Another effective self-compassion tool is called The Letter of Self-Compassion (explained in *The Neuroscience of Change*), which has been shown to decrease depression.[155] As you practice the skill of self-compassion, may you experience deeper levels of peace, comfort, and healing as a result. May the practice of these and other self-compassion exercises lead you down the road to unprecedented and long-lasting change.

CHAPTER 19

⊰⸻⊱

Recovering from Relapse[156]

Skill to Master #16: Minimizing self-criticism

Skill to Master #17: Self-forgiveness

Skill to Master #18: Rising quickly from perceived failures

In recovery, change is a process that never unfolds perfectly. As we learn the recovery lifestyle, it is essential to also learn how to respond if sobriety is compromised. Depending on the degree of our acting out behavior, this experience is referred to as a slip or a relapse. No matter how it is defined, a person's response to this kind of setback reveals the strength of their recovery process.

Shame is a normal feeling in moments of perceived failure. Self-criticism can naturally result from feelings of shame, yet a self-critical mindset decreases one's ability to successfully change and increases the chances of repeating the behavior and giving up.[157] Also, those who are more self-critical have less self-control and motivation.[158] Thus, it is unlikely that true change will occur when self-criticism remains the default manner of relating with oneself, especially in times of failure and weakness.[159]

On the other hand, a self-compassionate response, increases one's ability to get back on track quickly.[160] For those of us struggling with a shame-based identity, a perceived failure can quickly result in the desire to quit. Of course, quitting will not lead to lasting change. But strengthening the skill of responding self-compassionately to setbacks will powerfully propel us toward successful recovery.

Here is an example of how a person in recovery could self-compassionately respond to a slip or relapse, that supports connecting with self and with others:

Failure Response Worksheet[161]

Using a journal, answer the following:
- What triggered me to want to act out?
- What am I saying to myself about my behavior? (Words of self-criticism, shame, self-compassion?)

Practice a Self-Compassion Break:
- Close your eyes. Name all of the feelings you feel right now (example: guilt, shame, anger, sadness, disappointment, fear, etc.). Say to yourself "This is a moment of suffering." This is mindfulness.

- Common humanity (this is not meant to justify the choice but to normalize the feelings that result and to decrease shame, which is unproductive).
- Say to yourself the following phrases:
  "Suffering is a part of life."
  "Everyone makes mistakes sometimes when they are trying to make big changes."
  "My imperfections don't mean that something is wrong with me but only that I am human."
  "There are many people who feel this right now as a result of their choices."
- Now, put your hands over your heart, feel the warmth of your hands and feel yourself breathing (or use another gesture of soothing physical touch that is non-sexual). This gesture combined with kind words produces oxytocin – deepening a feeling of connection and comfort. For many, this will initially feel awkward but I urge you not to skip this significant step.
- Self-kindness message - Say to yourself the following phrases:
  "May I be kind to myself."
  "May I give myself the compassion that I need."
  "May I forgive myself."
  "May I be patient with myself."
  "May I be strong."
  "May I keep moving forward in my recovery."

Using a journal, answer the following:

- What tools can I use next time I am in a similar situation?

- How can I limit access to this form of acting out in the future?

Reach out to someone and tell them about your slip or relapse. Do this as soon as possible. Reconnect with your Higher Power and another human being. This decreases shame and secrecy, disempowering the addiction. Depending on the degree of damage to others, restitution and amends may be warranted. Sadly, we can never predict what pain or consequences will result from our choices. This is the risk of relapse. What we can control is our present response.

Repeatedly using this *Failure Response Worksheet* will train us to become our own supportive coach rather than a demoralizing critic. This can provide motivation to get up quickly and move forward, increasing the possibility of significant long-term changes.

While slips and relapses are disheartening, in recovery we learn to view them as opportunities for reconnection and learning, instead of excuses to chastise our efforts. We must remember that our worth is not weighed by success or failure. Our worth is innate, packaged in our humanity. Our mistakes don't define us but they do teach us about our process and our response to them is what matters most.[162]

Do you find yourself staring in the face of a recent failure? If so, this is the moment to act. Think about the inspiring scene from *Chariots of Fire* when Eric Liddell's race was interrupted with a sudden fall. The audience stood in awe and anticipation. When Eric rose, his determination was evident. In a burst of intensity, he swiftly restarted his sprint. The crowd cheered as he passionately pursued the finish line, passing all competitors in his path. To their amazement, he finished as the champion of the race. As he lay panting on the ground surrounded by runners and other bystanders, the officiate held Eric's head up, acknowledging the challenge of his run and the courage of his heart.

If you've fallen, be brave. Remember that "a setback only paves the way for a comeback."[163] Get up quickly. Practice self-compassion. Examine your blindspots. Reconnect with others. Forgive yourself. Finish your race and finish strong.

CHAPTER 20

———◆———

Pursuing Peace When the World's at War[164]

Skill to Master #19*: *Seeking and sustaining inner peace

Our world is in a frenzy of fear. Stories splash across our screens of both global and local terrorist attacks. We witness our world at war. Tragedies, in the forms of accidents and health risks, plague us. We witness a continual stream of messages that scream why we are unsafe in this world.

While we cannot change the uncertainty of the future, our response to this reality will either help or hurt humanity.

When external chaos breeds internal turmoil, we humans can make destructive decisions rooted in our mismanaged fears. In the words of Kristen Neff, "Oftentimes our reactions to these feelings are the most harmful, not the feelings themselves."[165]

Avoiding the escalation of hatred and violence in the world will necessitate the effective management of our fears. I believe this begins with our personal pursuit of peace.

A climactic scene from the movie *Kung Fu Panda 2* reflects the power of finding peace in the midst of scary situations. Po the Panda found himself in a frightening situation, standing alone on a rock, surrounded by water, with a powerful cannon pointed directly at him. As his enemy prepared to finish him, Po prepared his heart. He grounded himself. Po tapped into something deeper, something greater. When Po finally found his *inner peace*, he was empowered to endure the impossible. When the cannon balls boomed, he stood in his strength. The metal spheres made impact. Yet, instead of meeting his end, Po skillfully sent them back to sender. Po's surprising victory was rooted in the visceral calm he connected with. Similarly, when we experience internal peace, we too can stand our ground amidst the barrage of trials and temptations that torpedo toward us.

The pursuit of inner peace is particularly important for those of us recovering from addiction. We have a history of searching for peace in all the wrong places. We are skilled at calming ourselves by counterfeit means. We know how to numb. But in recovery, we learn to reach for what is real. We learn that peace that is packaged like pornography and decorated like drugs is illegitimate and illusory. Abandoning false paths to peace, we pursue authentic ones.

May all who long for peace in the midst of life's terrors and temptations consider the following avenues:

1. **Practice Gratitude** - In his helpful book *This is Your Brain On Joy,* Dr. Earl Henslin shares that according to the research "it is impossible to be grateful and loving

while also being fearful and angry."[166] When every day is Thanksgiving, we experience increased freedom from fear.

2. **Cultivate Self-Compassion** - In managing my own anxiety and working with clients, I have found Kristen Neff's *Self-Compassion Break* to be a potent passageway to peace (See Chapter 19 for a description of this exercise). When stress soars, investing in a few moments of self-compassion increases oxytocin, decreases cortisol, and helps us feel both soothed and safe.[167]

3. **Create Connection** - It is a true treasure when we find others who will respond to our distress in caring ways. Flores writes "regardless of our age or emotional development, we will always require some degree of emotional regulation from others. The denial of the need for others is what leads individuals to seek gratification (e.g., drugs, alcohol, food, sex, gambling, etc.) outside the realm of interpersonal relationships." When we are frozen in our fears, we can be warmed by the comfort of others.

4. **Strengthen the Soul** - Nothing calms fear quite like love.[168] This is one reason why spiritual connection is a potent source of peace. When we allow our hearts to be held, anxiety can decrease. Prayer, visualization, music, time in nature, and meditation aimed at strengthening attachment with a Higher Power in times of stress and distress can deepen a peaceful sense of security despite

outward circumstances. For many, spirituality also provides hope, strength, courage, and clarity.

As we individually pursue inner peace, our choices will change. Regardless of our political, cultural, and religious backgrounds, our responses to the worries of this world will prove more beneficial to everyone when grounded in calmness, courage, and connection.

Let there be peace on earth and let it begin with us.[169]

CHAPTER 21

The Time Travelers:
Making Changes that Matter[170]

<u>Skill to Master #20</u>: *Changing my present behavior as I connect with my future self*

Have you ever woken up with regret gnawing in your stomach? Do you think about your past choices with a strong resentment toward your past self? Those in recovery have countless experiences like this. Anyone who is trying to make significant changes understands that who they were in the past is the same person they are now, consequences included. But when it comes to looking ahead to the future, we are often disconnected from that reality, failing to imagine that our future self is actually *us*. We just haven't met them yet.

For those wishing to change their current behavior, this concept is essential. Dr. Kelly McGonigal talks about future self connection in detail sharing that, according to research, feeling separate from one's future self decreases one's protection of that future self's well-being.[171] Conversely, feeling connected to one's future self increases self-control.[172]

Think about it.

- What choices would you change if you had a deeper awareness and appreciation of this present/future self connection?
- Would you be more likely to create healthy habits now, teleporting the benefits to your older self who lives years ahead in the future?
- How would this affect your rituals of running into self-destructive situations?

Since we are more impulsive when we are oblivious to the future effects of our actions,[173] I wonder how often we forfeit future joy by making impulsive choices that *only* have apparent benefits in the present moment? Whether this means looking at pornography for hours to drown feelings of loneliness or eating a gallon of ice cream to temporarily alleviate difficult emotions, there are countless opportunities to make unhealthy choices with a blind eye to the future.

Now that the importance of the present connection with your future self is explained, you are likely wondering "how can I connect with my future self?" The answer is obvious, isn't it? *Time travel.* But since technology fails us in this area, let's consider some specific ways we can time travel, meeting the person we imagine ourselves to be in the future.

In the movie *X-Men: Days of Future Past,* the main character is teleported across time through his mind. Although we lack the superpower to literally do this, we can certainly use our imagination to *travel* to the future.

McGonigal recommends fostering this future self connection by writing a letter *from* yourself in the future *to* your current self.[174] Try this exercise:[175]

- Imagine being your future self 10 or 20 years from now.
- Write to your present self about the current challenges to overcome your sexual addiction and change the unhealthy lifestyle that accompanies it.
- Thank your present self for doing the hard work to overcome this addiction.
- Explain to your present self in detail *how* this was accomplished and *why* it was so significant. What ripple effects were the result of your recovery? How did your recovery impact your connections with yourself, your Higher Power, and those you love? How did your freedom inspire others impacted by their addictions and how did your recovery free you to impact the world for good? As you write, remain positive and hopeful.
- Give your present self encouragement and direction for the difficult path ahead.
- Read this letter to yourself in front of the mirror, record yourself reading it to play back to yourself regularly, or have someone else read it to you.
- Repeat this exercise daily or when your recovery commitments begin to fade.

Here's another future self connection exercise[176] you can practice (I suggest doing this under the guidance of a professional or skipping this if you are emotionally unstable):

- Close your eyes.
- Vividly imagine the future consequences of living an addicted, self-focused, self-neglectful, and disconnected life.
- Experience the feelings associated with *this* possible future reality.
- Then, vividly imagine the future benefits of living free from addiction and being deeply connected with yourself, your Higher Power, and with those you love.
- Experience the feelings associated with *this* possible future reality.
- Open your eyes.
- Take immediate positive action to start creating the future reality you want to experience.
- Reach out for support if triggered by this exercise.
- Repeat this exercise daily or when your recovery commitments begin to fade.

As you think about fostering friendship with your future self, remember that this type of self-connection can increase your investment in a more meaningful future.[177]

May these exercises infuse you with courage to *let go* of destructive habits that will damage your future self's reality and relationships. May these exercises motivate you to *grab onto* healthy habits now, however uncomfortable they may feel in the present, resulting in a lasting impact on your future reality.

May we all remember that our choices today create our tomorrow.

CHAPTER 22

Connected Sex: A Paradigm Shift for the Sexually Addicted[178]

Skill to Master #21: _Learning to emotionally connect with my partner_

Skill to Master #22: _Practicing a healthy, connected sexuality_

It may go without saying but sex is a significant topic for recovering sex addicts. As a sex addiction therapist, I tell my clients that successful recovery necessitates a new view of sexuality. Rather than seeing sex as a numbing agent, instead, sex in recovery is a connecting agent. This transition in thinking and practice is difficult, since sex addicts inherently have a dysfunctional relationship with sex, rooted in an intimacy disorder.

A Sex Addict's Sex Life

There are many ways in which a sex addict's perception of sex is distorted and unhealthy. In her TEDx Talk on Sex and Intimacy, Dr. Sue Johnson superbly explained the dynamics of connected and disconnected sex.[179] Her explanation of *sealed off sex* is characteristic of the sex addict's experience because it lacks emotional intimacy, is solely sensation and performance focused, and leaves individuals feeling lonely. Sex addicts may also seek out *solace sex*, where the focus is on reassurance rather than sexual passion.[180] The significance of both of these sex styles is that they are rooted in insecure attachment patterns,[181] which are common among sex addicts. [182] Dr. Linda Hatch similarly describes the sex life of sex addicts, writing:

> *Even when the sex addict is having sex with a partner or spouse, it is often the case that the addict is not "all there." He or she may be lost in fantasy or just going through the motions. Many addicts feel they are having satisfying sex with their partners when in fact they are not really able to be present.*[183]

I often describe this dynamic to my clients as "using your partner to masturbate." Sex for the sex addict is an experience of emotional *disconnection*. The sex addict sees sex as a drug and distraction, not a profound point of *connection*. The sex addict hijacks sexuality to get their self-focused high.[184] This distorts the very purpose of the sexual experience.

Sex for the sex addict is lust-driven, not love-driven. Regardless of whether a sex addict objectifies a stranger or their partner, connection never results.[185]

Another pattern that some sex addicts experience is called *sexual anorexia*, which occurs when a person avoids sex and emotional connection completely. [186] Alexandra Katehakis explains that "where sex addicts 'act out' or 'binge' through promiscuity or high-risk behavior, sexual anorexics starve themselves by 'acting in,' denying themselves the pleasure of relationships, dating, loving touch, and genuine connection with others."[187] Sometimes, both *acting out* and *acting in* dynamics are at play, creating a *sexual bulimic* like cycle of sexual binging and purging.[188]

As you can see, there are many potential scenarios that explain the sex addict's misguided use of sex. Difficulties ensue when sex is used solely for coping, not connecting.

All About Intimacy

In their book *The Couple's Guide to Intimacy*, Drs. Bill and Ginger Bercaw explain that "one of the greatest challenges facing couples in recovery is learning how to be emotionally and sexually intimate after the relationship has absorbed a direct hit."[189] A couple reeling from this type of relational trauma has a lot of hard work ahead.

As recovery progresses, sex addicts have the opportunity to see sex with new eyes. They can learn to appreciate a depth to sex they never knew before, experiencing what Katehakis describes as the "sensuality of connected closeness."[190] Connected sex, or *synchrony sex*, is a bonding experience that includes openness, play, and sexual passion.[191] As connected sex becomes a new ideal, the addict will find that this transformation requires something quite unexpected: a foundation of emotional connection. This is the key to a quality sexual relationship.[192]

The core of good sex is safety and connection, but these are two areas in which sex addicts experience extreme deficiencies. Most couples working toward fostering emotional intimacy will need extensive work with an attachment-based sex addiction therapist. Learning to deeply connect with their partner is an essential skill for sexual addicts in recovery.

This type of learning requires guidance, work, and a plethora of patience, but with the right help there is hope. Active recovery is necessary for any couple working toward increased connection. If the addict is engaging in their acting-out behaviors, the addiction becomes a *competing attachment*, [193] hindering the couple's closeness. Thus, sobriety is a starting line for the couple's successful connection journey.

Often recovering sex addicts, whether in a relationship or single, abstain from masturbation as part of their sobriety. This makes more sense when sex is seen as a connecting experience rather than a solo act. When masturbation is lust-driven, compulsive, or sought out for emotional comfort, this behavior plays a key role in the addictive cycle. Still, there are varying views on the topic of masturbation in recovery, [194] which is another reason why seeking guidance from a sex addiction therapist is recommended.

In early recovery, it is common for sex addiction therapists to prescribe a period of sexual celibacy from all expressions of sexuality, including with their partner. This orchestrated season of abstinence can have many benefits for the addict, partner, and couple, including taking the "sexual pressure off of the relationship so the couple can work on play and communication." This period can offer a detox from unhealthy and unhelpful beliefs about sex, clearing the way for other forms of connection.

On the pathway to connected sexuality, there may be many detours. Sexual abuse, sexual dysfunction, medical issues, distrust, trauma, and other factors may complicate the couple's sexual experience, requiring additional help from a sex therapist, doctor, or other professional. Patterns of sexual avoidance grounded in a partner's lack of emotional safety or using sex as an attempt to control the addict's behavior should be addressed with a sex addiction therapist.

The Powerful Potential of Connected Sex

When a sex addict learns to experience sex as the "potent bonding activity"[195] it can be, this is a massive mental shift for them. Instead of using sex as a drug: to escape, numb, or avoid, sex can become a source of satisfaction. Healing from a shame-based sexuality will be part of the process. Learning how to leave lust and objectification out of the bedroom are additional aims of recovery.

The truth is, all connection work in recovery, whether emotional or sexual, will require the help of those who know the way. The Bercaws' book is an excellent resource for couples impacted by sex addiction. I love the vision they cast of what a recovered sex life can look like:

> *You can know for perhaps the first time in your entire life what it feels like to embrace a passionate and fully satisfying sex life while retaining your integrity and while being more fully present.*[196]

Katehakis casts a similar vision of healthy sexuality, calling it "a profoundly new experience. It has the ring of innocence and simplicity, devoid of addictive adrenalized and dopaminergic intensity. For the first time, the psyche and body do not melt in disarray afterward. Healthy sex can make amends to the self and to the partner. When partners join in an open-hearted and present way, sex becomes a genuine act of love in the moment and leaves both parties feeling good afterward."[197]

Imagine that: A shame-free sexuality. A satisfying experience of secret-free sex based on love. This is what lust always promised but never delivered.

Dr. Mark Laaser tells a story of one recovering couple who experienced non-addictive sex for the first time.[198] Their time together ended in a loving embrace and joyful tears. This is the prospect of connected sexuality.

As we grow in our willingness to challenge and change our distorted views of sex, we can learn to experience a more fulfilling, connected, and healthy sexuality. A paradigm shift is possible.

CHAPTER 23

What's Your Recovery Anthem?[199]

__Skill to Master #23__: Connecting with my values

__Skill to Master #24__: Prioritizing important relationships

---

What's your *recovery anthem*? You know, *the* song that inspires you to rise higher and fight harder?

A *recovery anthem* is highly personal. The song that speaks to you may not speak to me. Some songs stir us more deeply than others, based on our beliefs and backgrounds. Oftentimes, our anthem finds us when we are most desperate for reassurance and strength.

For me, a song worthy to be hailed as a *recovery anthem* must be one that courses through my veins, stirs up emotion, calls me to action, increases my passion, and raises my intention to both battle and heal. I have created playlists of such songs in the past.

Yesterday, I found my newest *recovery anthem*. How did I know this was *my* song? One hint was that it repeatedly brought me to tears. It also gave me a wider perspective and increased the intensity of my commitment.

I would like to share my anthem with you. Maybe it will profoundly speak to you. Maybe not. Regardless, my hope is that it will inspire you to find your own *recovery anthem*.

My Recovery Anthem

My new *recovery anthem* is the song *If the House Burns Down Tonight* by the band Switchfoot. The lyrics resonate deeply with me, as I think about the prospect of fighting for love and letting everything else burn away.

To me, this means passionately pursuing my relationship with God. This means deepening my loyal love for my bride. This means daily communicating my affection to my kids. This means prioritizing the love of my family and friends. This means holding onto love while letting all of the distractions, addictions, and meaningless attempts to impress anyone or prove anything burn away. This means loving like that and letting others love me in the same way.

In real recovery we find the commitment and courage to fiercely hold onto those things we value the most, abandoning everything that competes for life's most precious gift: love.

I invite you to invest a few minutes in listening to Switchfoot's song. Imagine the love you want to pursue and what you're willing to give up to get it.

Find Your Anthem

Start looking for your personal *recovery anthem*. Our *recovery anthem* sparks strength in us when we feel depleted and ignites hope within when we feel defeated. We can listen to our *recovery anthem* daily and in times of urgent need.

The *recovery anthem* is a powerful tool for those seeking recovery from anything.

What's your *recovery anthem*? I would love to hear it.

CHAPTER 24

How Paying Attention Protects
Our Children from Porn

---

*Skill to Master #25: Learning to pay attention to my children,
fostering deeper connection*

The discovery of a child's first pornography exposure is every parent's nightmare. Yet I have heard enough stories and done enough research to believe that all parents will experience this frightening future moment. Whether accidentally or intentionally, I believe every child will see pornography. It's not a matter of *if* but *when* they are exposed, regardless of their gender, background, or beliefs.

Some would call that "bad news." I call it reality. The hopeful side of this reality is that by *paying attention* to our children in four specific ways, we as parents can prepare our children's hearts and protect our children's eyes, limiting the impact of an inevitable exposure to pornography.

May we all as parents learn to pay attention to our children in these four crucial ways:

1. **<u>Pay attention to their access.</u>** We exhibit wisdom when we are aware of the porn-accessing potential of every device used by our children. Not only can we research the capabilities of this technology but also put up protective programs to limit inappropriate content. By doing so, we minimize the potential for pornography exposure in our home. This requires both initial efforts and long-term diligence, as the limits of these protections are tested. But paying attention in this way will spare our children from unlimited access to the worst of the web.

2. **<u>Pay attention to their habits.</u>** When we observe the routines of our children, we remain alert to changes in behavior. We are tuned in to attitudes and actions that serve as red flags that pornography is being pursued by our children. These changes could include an increase in tiredness, lying, or other suspicious behavior. If our child has secretly accessed pornography, our awareness of their habits helps us more quickly intervene, assisting them by closing any open doors to porn as quickly as possible.

3. **<u>Pay attention to their interests.</u>** When we are actively engaged in our children's daily activities, a more trusting relationship can develop. More time together means

145

more conversations. When we are willing to disengage from our distractions, pursuing interested involvement with our children, the relational bond is deepened. When our children eventually access pornography, they will be more likely to share their struggles with us when we are consistent in caring about their interests, desires, and needs.

4. **Pay attention to their emotions.** When we as parents are attuned and responsive to our children's emotional states, we lay the groundwork for secure attachment. Of all the factors that can protect our children from a long-term vulnerability to addiction, this is the most prominent. When our children are securely attached to us, they learn to regulate their emotions through relationship. When we fail to respond enough to our children's emotions, this is emotional neglect.[200] Many adult sexual addicts were emotionally neglected[201] as children. They were taught not to trust relational comfort, learning instead to self-soothe in sexually addictive ways.[202] Our journey of learning to connect with our children may entail reading books, seeking treatment for our own addictions and mental distractions, and practicing new skills. Learning to effectively pay attention to our children's emotional life will prove to powerfully protect them from pornography addiction, in both the present and far into the future.

Paying attention to our children not only helps protect them from pornography but from a host of lifetime problems. Let's face it; life is hard. How we steward our relationship with our children will either increase or subtract from their suffering in life. Though our efforts cannot guarantee healthy futures for our children, we can still give them the best foundation we can for making healthy choices.

No matter how old they are, our children deserve parents who are willing to invest the necessary time it takes to pay attention and to care. To do this, we must unplug from our own distractions, whether we are sucked into our screens or continually looking out for lust. It will take intentionality on our part and we will need support along the way. But few things satisfy like knowing we gave our best efforts, raising children that not only resist the pull of pornography but who live to love others, changing a world that is captivated by lust.

CHAPTER 25

Holiday Recipes for Relapse and Recovery[203]

Skill to Master #26*: Maintaining recovery structure and self-care over the holidays*

For those who have other religious or holiday traditions, this material may translate to any special occasions observed by the reader.

The holidays can feel like a minefield for those in recovery. More so than other times of the year, potentially disastrous dynamics go hand-in-hand with the celebrations of the season. Sexual addicts can benefit from preparing themselves for the inherent holiday challenges by understanding the following recipes for relapse and recovery. May these compelling reminders provide guidance for all who hope to maintain momentum through the holiday season.

Recipes for Relapse:

1. **Increased triggers.** The holidays often contain plentiful triggers. There can be triggers related to specific days and places that remind addicts of past acting out or trauma. Interactions with relatives can ignite internal suffering, whether through family drama or reminders of past losses. New or different environments can be triggers, especially when the drug of choice is suddenly made available. Additionally, the attitude of indulgence that often accompanies the holidays can lead to all-or-nothing thinking that increases addictive and self-defeating behaviors.

2. **Decreased structure.** Addiction thrives in disorder. The structure of recovery (i.e. maintaining healthy habits, minimizing of triggers, connecting with accountability, attending meetings, etc.) offers safety for those striving not to slip. Addiction counselor Jim LaPierre emphasizes the importance of maintaining structure and recovery routines, sharing that an addict with too much free time is an addict in a dangerous situation.[204] Time off work and/or school combined with little to no responsibility can be disorienting for those in recovery. Boredom, laziness with recovery routines, and feeling an overall lack of constraint can quickly lead addicts into preoccupation and relapse.

3. **Food and sugar...everywhere!** The majority of popular American holidays have a large sugar component. Whether in the plethora of pumpkin pies at Thanksgiving, the convenience of Christmas candies, or the excess of Easter sweets, sugar is significant. Self-control is necessary for recovering addicts; unfortunately, high sugar consumption results in increased impulsivity.[205] Additionally, using food to cope with the many holiday stressors may offer temporary numbness but does not result in the connection (with self and others) that is intrinsic in successful recovery. Of course, we can enjoy the delicious delicacies of the season but when we find ourselves eating to escape or seeking out "comfort foods" to manage our moods, we are entering addictive territory.

Recipes for Recovery:

1. **Sustaining self-care.** Self-care is inseparable from successful recovery and the holidays are no exception. Maintaining habits that strengthen the brake system of the brain (the pre-frontal cortex) results in an infusion of strength and self-control. Sleep, exercise, healthy eating, and mindful breathing all have this empowering effect in the brain. [206] Making time for relaxation and the enjoyment of fun activities is not only essential for recovery but also for experiencing the joys of living. Making food choices that avoid crashes and promote consistent energy can be helpful. [207] Starting with morning inspiration and ending with healthy evening decompression will be especially important. All of these

self-care practices create needed structure and will aid in sustaining recovery throughout the holiday season.

2. **Remaining connected.** Strength and stability are rooted in connection. Reaching out to one's accountability team, spouse or partner, friends, sponsor, and Higher Power can help those in recovery stay grounded, managing emotions and other triggers.

   Connection to self is also vital. Maintaining an intimate understanding of what's happening internally can help with decisions to take breaks for much-needed down-time. Being aware of imminent needs is essential for those in recovery. When experiencing emotional suffering inherent in interactions with others or resulting from personal choices, a self-compassion practice is recommended.

   While maintaining these connections are especially helpful for relapse prevention, they can also help those in recovery recommit quickly after perceived mistakes or slips before the addictive behavior escalates.

3. **Maintaining mindfulness.** It is impossible to be mindful and compulsive simultaneously. Those in recovery may find themselves in diverse and unexpected circumstances and mindfulness helps protect against unhelpful reactivity. Surfing the Urge[208] is a great tool that stops overreaction to inner turmoil and the impulsive indulgence of cravings. Being mindful of both your external environment and your internal landscape (i.e. feelings, triggers, cravings, etc.) will help sexual addicts make wiser choices and more fully enjoy each moment.

Savoring Success

Staying committed and successful requires sustained effort. Baking up these recipes for recovery may feel burdensome. While time-intensive, those who invest in these strategies will experience just the opposite. This much-needed structure promotes true freedom and enjoyment.

Keeping in mind the purpose of these strategies and personal reasons for staying committed will help those in recovery remain on track with their goals. This proactive approach to surviving the holidays will result in refreshment, end in energy, and supercharge connections. Those who practice these principles will savor the satisfying aroma of accomplishment, with an acute awareness that they cooked up something meaningful in the midst of challenging conditions.

CHAPTER 26

———◆———

Four Strategies for a Successful Summer Vacation[209]

**Skill to Master #27**: Maintaining recovery structure and self-care on vacation

**Skill to Master #28**: Making worthy memories

**Skill to Master #29**: Learning to have fun apart from addiction

---

Summer is often a season of travel and time away from regular responsibilities. For those of us in recovery, vacations can be filled with new temptations and triggers. When we neglect our recovery routines and indulge in everything our eyes desire, we dance with danger.

Vacations are vulnerable times for me. I've experienced first-hand how late nights and lack of structure can quickly lead to lust binges and weakened self-control. I can too quickly slip into states of self-neglect and disconnect when I do not remain intentional in my recovery work. For those who experience similar vulnerabilities on vacation, here are four strategies for success:

1. **Plan and scan.** With new environments come new temptations and triggers. Whenever possible, plan ahead for these. Scan new scenery for situations that could take you out. Alert your accountability partners to emerging challenges, communicating your proactive plan to evade them. Rather than being a victim to vulnerable circumstances, remain responsible, mindful, and vigilant.

2. **Stay connected.** Avoid behaviors and experiences that disconnect you from those you love, including yourself. Stay connected to your feelings, your values, your accountability, your spiritual strength, and those around you. Celebrate in such a way that your future self will thank you, not resent you.

3. **Care for yourself.** Remain faithful to your self-care structures, remembering that while there is an obvious vacation from regular schedules and responsibilities, there is never a vacation from essential recovery routines. Self-care may include seeking solitude and healthy self-soothing when triggered or over-stimulated.

4. **Make meaningful memories.** Recovery is not just about avoiding self-destruction but also about the construction of a full life. This too takes intentionality. Learning how

to have fun without lust, excessive sugar, and other drugs of choice is a significant challenge of recovery. Investing in guilt-free memories with those we love will lay the foundation of a new and meaningful life.

Remember, your proactive plan also protects your partner. If they know you are actively engaged in recovery, whether on the road or at home, their sense of safety is strengthened. May those who travel experience many moments of heartfelt goodbyes and honorable returns, fostering deep reconnection. May we all enjoy many satisfying summers strengthened by solid recovery.

CHAPTER 27

———◆———

A Connected Christmas: Avoiding Auto-Pilot and Making Today Meaningful[210]

Skill to Master #30*: Connecting with my reasons for fighting for my recovery*

Skill to Master #31*: Preparing for potential temptations*

For those who have other religious or holiday traditions, this material may translate to any special occasions observed by the reader.

Christmas is a day of celebration, gratitude, and connection....at least in theory. I desire these ideals yet too often find myself indulgent and disconnected. Vacations and holidays are historically hard for me. So often self-care slumps, discipline diminishes, and disconnection dominates. These tendencies are my auto-pilot.

I imagine there are many who start their Christmas day with the seemingly inevitable indulgences staring them down. Whether it's the almost unavoidable spreads of sugar or numerous other numbing experiences, we all have vices that lure our hearts away from meaningful connection. Yet, we still have choices.

Last year, I found myself headed toward that familiar highway to hedonism. I thought, "here we go again," believing I was cementing a course for the holidays that would leave me disappointed and dissatisfied.

What happened next changed everything.

I made two moves that turned my heart back to mindfulness and connection.

First, I reached out. I told those I trusted about the temptations that were tugging at me. Then I did something new, something that immediately turned the tables, infusing me with strength and purpose.

I left myself a voicemail.

Not just any voicemail.

This was a message to myself that I had crafted previously. I created this powerful message for moments of disconnection; for anticipated moral emergencies when I knew I was starting to stray. In this message, I shared vivid imagery and meaningful metaphors. I used song lyrics, spiritual symbols, memories of strength and victory, truths I have learned, etc. Basically, I pulled out the *big guns*, communicating everything I knew that would reconnect me with my purpose and that which I hold most dear.

My message to myself included the following phrases:

Forest, you are a faithful husband who is committed to connection. You are a loving father, committed to modeling faith and trust to your kids. You've committed to them that you will seek connection and reject addiction. You are a husband who promised on your wedding day to pursue your wife, not lust.

You are a therapist and teacher who represents other professionals and seeks to inspire others who are also fighting alongside you today.

You are not alone.

Play with all your heart today.

Today, your engagement in life and connection to God can be an inspiration to others. I know you will choose self-love today. Focus also on loving your family extravagantly, avoiding selfishness. Take care of your body today, feed it in a way that will give you energy and self-confidence. Protect your mind today and fill it with worthy thoughts. Remember your worthy goals to impact the world for good. Be strong and courageous, looking for divine moments, not slipping into passivity.

Let your vacation be fun, relaxing, and joyful but remember that you are not on vacation from your recovery. May this Christmas be a time of growth and greatness.

I spoke this passionate message to myself against the backdrop of a song that always infuses me with strength and a warrior-like attitude. Once I recorded this voicemail and listened to it, that's exactly what I had.

It carried me through Christmas Eve. I felt connected and in control. I ended the day without regrets.

On Christmas morning, I listened to the voicemail again, with the same effect. It infused me with power, focus, and connection. I anticipated a great day of celebration, gratitude, and connection.

For those interested in making their own message, here are some guiding questions:

1. What are my recovery and growth goals for this holiday season?
2. What are some motivating memories that remind me why I'm committed to recovery?
3. What are my dreams and values?
4. What music, video clips, or quotes inspire me to live a more meaningful life?
5. What symbols or imagery remind me of my greater purpose?
6. What signs and triggers might I experience today that will remind me to take a break, practice self-care, and listen to my voicemail again?

Now write a paragraph to yourself based on your answers. Remember, that shaming yourself will not lead to change, but a self-compassionate and encouraging message can infuse you with strength.

Next, call yourself, sincerely speaking your message. You can even ask those who care about you (like your partner, friends, or accountability group members) to leave you additional encouraging messages. Then, save these inspirational pep-talks for the future moments when you'll need them.

May we all invest the time to connect with what matters most to us. May it make all the difference, as we experience the joy of a connected Christmas. Re-connection is always possible...even in this very moment.

CHAPTER 28

Three Tales of Temptation

<u>Skill to Master #32</u>: Connecting with the legitimate needs driving my addictive cravings

<u>Skill to Master #33</u>: Learning to ask for what I need

<u>Skill to Master #34</u>: Practicing the recovery principle of "one day at a time"

I wish I knew what triggered me that night. Maybe it was a long, tiring day. Possibly I was sleep-starved or simply drained. Whatever preceded my preoccupation, I was on the hunt for pornography.

Deciding to buy a magazine, I entered a Kwik-E-Mart style store. Anytime I'd arrive at a public place with impure motives, my ritual included scanning the store for anyone I knew. Only in the absence of acquaintances would I pursue pornography. Then, I believed I was getting away with it. After all, the behavior I planned grated against my conscience and values. It was not who I wanted to be.

Suddenly, someone I knew walked in. It was a woman from my church college group. I could've taken this as a sign to stop in my tracks. I could've grabbed some gum and started a conversation. But that was the last thing I wanted. Beet red, heart-pounding, I hid from sight in the back of the store. At an opportune time I exited the building, too embarrassed to buy anything.

That night, I visited a few locations before finding both the indecent images and the courage to buy them. A pile of candy accompanied my magazine purchase. This was important for two reasons:

1. To mix my two favorite drugs.
2. To conceal the lust-driven reality that I really just wanted the porn. Don't think I fooled anyone.

Dead-set on acting out privately, I did something unheard of. I knew I took a risk bringing my pornographic purchase home. There was a chance my roommates might try to derail me. Heaven forbid they catch me in my murky motives or call me up out of the mud. So, I splurged on a hotel room. There I was guaranteed all the uninterrupted self-indulgence I desired.

That night I both acted out and pigged out. I watched MTV and did what I wanted.

Then I took a hot bath. Soaking in the tub, I finally relaxed. I realized the bath was what I had needed all along. All the addictive gratification that left me feeling spiritually ashamed and physically sick wasted my time, life, and money. Yet, in that season, all I knew was compulsive comfort. I was lost in the fight against lust. When emotionally exhausted, I'd escape into the sexual coping I'd practiced since childhood. It never met my needs but I kept coming back for more of the same and more of the shame. Abandoning my real needs, I just numbed myself with lust. Trapped in this self-defeating cycle, I could never heal.

Fast forward fourteen years.

I was married with children and pornography use was a thing of the past. We were out of town for Christmas and I found myself in a fog of tiredness. I was feeling the affect of too many sweets and not enough sleep. Despite my better judgment, I started playing with fire, stealthily scanning through TV channels, looking for something lust-inducing. While I knew pornography was off the table, there were lesser forms of lust that I foolishly justified. Then I found something to feed my "need" to numb: movie channels.

Movie channels and I went way back. I recall countless childhood memories of seeking out uncensored movies. The adrenaline rush of sneakiness coupled with the lure of lust was the continual high of my young years. Talk about a trigger. This little secret could quickly sabotage my sobriety and self-worth. I was on dangerous ground.

Soon after this discovery my wife returned from an errand. Angered by her tardiness and ingratitude, I began desiring deeper rebelliousness. One thing worse than experiencing a trigger is experiencing *layers* of triggers simultaneously.

Tiredness.

Sugared-up.

An open door to easy lust.

Resentment.

It was an explosive combination. I was on a short road to relapse. Or so it seemed.

I am a strong believer that we are never destined to lose our sobriety. Even when we slack in healthy habits and stack the deck against ourselves, our recovery is our responsibility. We are more than mere moths floating toward alluring flames.

In that fateful moment, I chose to take a time out. Seeking solitude, I somehow summoned the strength to call my voicemail. It was there that I had prepared a motivating message for myself in anticipation of possible temptations. There I heard the challenge of my own voice saying, "Forest, thank you for calling. Remember to have self-compassion today. Remember who you are." Hearing those words and the ones that followed ignited me with enough initiative to send out an emergency text to my band of brothers. Then I prayed, requesting God's rescue.

The idea came to me to take a hot bath. Asking for some alone time, I was relieved by my wife's support. Soaking in the warm water, I read the *White Book of Sexaholics Anonymous*. In another loving gesture, my wife surprised me with two lit candles. Resting in the tub, I relished in the luminous light cascading across the darkened room. As I read about *A Loving God Who Knows and Cares*, I felt a Divine presence bringing me back to my higher senses. Hearing the voices of my sweet boys in another room, I thought about them, remembering my commitment to fight for my freedom on their behalf. Before ending my time in the tub, I intentionally inhaled the lingering love around me, exhaling the lust that no longer mastered me.

Rewind two years.

Whose bright idea was it to hold an addiction conference in Vegas? Though the idea was laughable, I hoped to attend. The million-dollar question was "how could I go and not crash in my recovery?" I thoughtfully decided I could make the trip while managing my recovery, knowing that to do so I would need to grow my game to the next level.

At the time, I was reading *The Willpower Instinct* by Dr. Kelly McGonigal. She wrote about the advertising tactics used to boost dopamine, increasing impulsivity of potential buyers. This primed me to guard against the sounds, smells, lights and sights that would constantly compete for my attention in Sin City.

In preparation, I did all I knew to do. I visualized my return to the airport, my future self's excitement and affirmation as I de-boarded in victory. I prepared my accountability partner, planning to continually check-in with him. Setting up a schedule to Skype with my family, I readied myself to remain connected.

Knowing I would need to have fun, I brought a movie I wanted to watch. My morning routines would include exercise, prayer, and recovery inspiration. My diet would be sugar-free and sleep would be a priority. If the hotel would not respect my request to remove the TV, I would cover it, committing not to turn it on. My family picture would be placed in front of it.

My lofty goal for the trip was abstaining from *all* lust. Some would call this perfectionistic. To me, it was die-hard commitment. I was going to create and experience life after lust.

I finally lifted off to Las Vegas. From start to finish, I executed my recovery plan. While there were many "opportunities" to glide into lust, I stayed the course. This trip became for me far more than just maintaining sobriety; I lived my recovery. I connected with others at the convention while maintaining connections to my loved ones at home. I remained aligned to my values and followed my recovery roadmap. I experienced joy, awe, and adventure.

The trip was not without potential paths to wander away from commitments. At one point, when walking from my hotel, I saw a pornographic magazine on the ground. Feeling strong enough to protect others, I bent down while looking up and away, grabbed the magazine and stuffed it deep into a nearby bush. In my mind, it led to one less child potentially exposed to pornography. I was also aware of the allure of free sugary foods, like the white and dark chocolate fondue fountains. I resisted their mouth-watering magnetism.

When the trip was finally finished and I de-planed in my home city, I envisioned my future self meeting me at my gate in a jovial spirit of celebration and excitement. I had thrived in the midst of many temptations, finishing the entire trip lust free.

Lessons Learned from Lust and Life

Looking back, I see enduring wisdom in this series of stories. I have learned so much in a lifetime of battling lust. I've tasted the tears of temporary defeat and hard-fought triumph. I've also tasted life after lust and vouch for the fulfillment I've found in those victories.

I wish I could say that my big recovery successes led to permanent power over lust. You may have noticed that these stories were not in chronological order. After the high of living aligned in Las Vegas, I somehow returned to passive recovery. The lesson I extract from that is this: Yesterday's achievements can infuse me with inspiration but cannot guarantee today's triumph. If I assume I've arrived, I will let my guard down, making myself susceptible to struggles.

Does that mean that the drive to act out doesn't decrease over time? With consistent work, it does decrease. As we learn to reach toward love instead of lust, our brains get rewired. The old life becomes unnatural. But for long-term recovery from lust to endure, it must be maintained. Having mastered the practices that led us here, we live them out the rest of our life. We cannot afford apathy in our recovery. The newbie and the veteran alike must live by the axiom "one day at a time."

Part 3

Mission

When speaking publicly to teenagers about pornography, I begin by asking them, "What plans do you have for your life?" They call out their hopes for career and college. They mention marriage. Then I follow-up asking, "What if your porn use could get in the way of those plans? How hard would you fight for your freedom?"

This is much more than mere scare tactics. I aim to raise their awareness that pornography addiction can seriously sever them from future success. I could tell of countless men and women who can vouch for such devastation in their own lives. We all face potential losses when sexual addiction has free reign in our lives.

Maybe you wish you received a similar warning when you were a teenager. While we cannot go back, we can look forward. Let us wisely consider the ramifications of our current choices. Will we sit idly by while time ticks away, hoping to change, yet failing to invest in the future of our dreams? Or will we look ahead with anticipation, feeding our hunger for healing and acting accordingly?

Addiction impairs our ability to make an impact on the world. In shame, we shrink back from life, rather than engaging in it. We lack faith in ourselves. We feel we've disappointed our Divine relationship.

In recovery, we connect deeply with ourselves. Our childhood dreams and desires are reawakened. We reevaluate our values. The more freedom we experience in recovery, the freer we are to live out our individual missions. We don't just recover to sit on the sidelines but to make a courageous contribution to the world. We are healed for a purpose.

In this section, I will share ways this has played out in my own life. These stories aim to inspire. There are specific battles that I believe in and I'll invite you to join in the ranks.

I also respect your discovery of personal destiny. As we grow, so too will our awareness of worthwhile ways to serve our world. We will learn how to leave a lasting legacy. These investments may include:

- Connecting with our kids in ways our parents never could.
- Crafting unprecedented intimacy in our romantic relationship.
- Shouldering the responsibility of becoming a mentor or sponsor.
- Watching the ripple effects when we boldly shine as our true selves.

In this section, you will be challenged to pursue the following *Missions to Accomplish* in your recovery journey:

Mission to Accomplish #1: Finding my purpose as I recover from my pain

Mission to Accomplish #2: Sustaining recovery with the hope of a meaningful future in mind

Mission to Accomplish #3: Standing against businesses that profit from the porn industry

Mission to Accomplish #4: Opposing the porn industry in my streets, my home, and my heart

Mission to Accomplish #5: Promoting the cause of love through the way I live my life

Mission to Accomplish #6: Finding the courage to stand for my deepest convictions

Mission to Accomplish #7: Standing against objectification and sexual exploitation

Mission to Accomplish #8: Actively working to raise my community's standards regarding all forms of pornography

Mission to Accomplish #9: Learning to live in alignment with my values

Mission to Accomplish #10: Maintaining a connected relationship with my children

Mission to Accomplish #11: Proactively protecting my children from the threats of pornography

Mission to Accomplish #12: Proactively protecting the younger generation from the threats of pornography

Mission to Accomplish 13: Waking up and taking action when my recovery commitments begin to wane

Mission to Accomplish #14: Maintaining long-term recovery

Mission to Accomplish #15: Creating a legacy for future generations

As we recover, our most meaningful contributions won't be measured through amassed personal achievements or popular votes. The values forged from our victories will be our greatest gifts to others. They will hitch-hike through generations, packaged as memories of the men and women we became: those who lived authentically and loved courageously. We won't be perfect but we will be present, passing on more of what matters. Our legacy will live on.

As we grow out of old habits, may we grow into the new. As we connect more fully with ourselves and others, we will feel empowered to encourage others, to serve, to give back. As we all long for liberty, may we look to a hopeful future, doing everything in our power to move forward and create it.

CHAPTER 29

———◆———◆———

Out of Our Pain Comes Our Purpose[211]

Mission to Accomplish #1: Finding my purpose as I recover from my pain

Mission to Accomplish #2: Sustaining recovery with the hope of a meaningful future in mind

---

> *"The two most important days in your life are the day you are born and the day you find out why." - Anonymous*

Over a decade ago I checked into a treatment program hoping to heal from a serious sexual addiction. A transformed life was Plan A. Plan B was a secret plot to escape to Las Vegas and drown myself in addictive self-destruction. My contingency plan never materialized because Plan A became my life's mission. Ironically, my recovery path recently led me back to Las Vegas. I was not there to indulge an addiction but to train therapists to treat those who do. This is one of many mind-blowing miracles I've savored in my recovery. Out of my past pain has come my present purpose. This is the hope of healing.

When we are deep in addiction and trauma, we are blind to future hope. We cannot imagine living in the light when we feel lost in the night. It takes a bold imagination to take steps forward in recovery when we can't predict where that path will take us.

I cannot tell you where your recovery path will take you but I believe one thing: Out of your pain will come your purpose. Healing is about far more than just managing triggers, but about stepping into a meaningful life. When we are no longer handcuffed by our impulses, we are free to love and live more fully. This is my experience. I believe it can be yours as well.

Are you willing to do the deep and difficult work of recovery today, holding tightly to the belief that you will benefit tomorrow?

Are you willing to postpone present pleasure and persevere through present pain for the promise of future satisfaction?

If you answer "yes" then I welcome you to a courageous journey of faith. Here we begin to believe in the unseen. We imagine a different future while persistently pursuing it. When our purposeful future finds us, we will truly see that we've sacrificed nothing and gained everything. We wrestled for our recovery and it was worth it. We were healed for a purpose.

CHAPTER 30

———◆———

Vote for Love[212]

Mission to Accomplish #3: Standing against businesses that profit from the porn industry

Mission to Accomplish #4: Opposing the porn industry in my streets, my home, and my heart

Mission to Accomplish #5: Promoting the cause of love through the way I live my life

---

In 2016, I read about Hustler's plan to open a store in my city. Standing on my values, I wrote the following article to local citizens, which was published on LifeSTARCentralValley.wordpress.com and in The Fresno Bee newspaper.

With elections on everyone's minds, this is a season when every vote matters. While we focus on polls and politics, another local election looms. Recent news just revealed Hustler's hopes to put up shop in our city. If they come, we will cast votes with our cash on our community's stance on pornography. As this porn industry giant petitions for our votes, I wonder how many will grant their stamp of approval, disguised as dollars.

Supposedly, the majority of their merchandise will not be porn related. In one article, the company president framed this as a retail operation, with a fraction of "adult" content. To me, this is exponentially more deceptive. Even if a customer exits the store with G-rated clothing, they unknowingly cast their vote for a successful porn industry.

I can't do that.

Gassing up at a station that peddles porn may not register as wrong. But I have resisted this for years, regardless of price. I have also often avoided buying from a local big-name bookstore because their explicit books are visible to adolescent eyes. I've long bypassed convenient coffee and the best looking burgers when sold to the public through seduction. I know I vote with every transaction; supporting a porn selling business means supporting the porn industry. I refuse to give them my stamp of approval.

As a sexual addiction therapist, I continuously see the devastation caused by porn addiction. I sit with stunned spouses. I empathize with addicts caught in self-destructive cycles. I help resuscitate relationships ruined by pornographic obsessions and aid in the burial of relationships wounded beyond repair.

As a presenter on the harmful effects of porn, I see a younger generation that's predominantly unprotected from it. I see our youth unknowingly auctioning off present and future intimacy as they immerse themselves in the internet. Porn changes their malleable brains,[213] affecting everything from their studying to later-life sexual performance.[214] Many are drowning in addiction. I do my best to protect my children from this destructive drug.

As a sexual addict in recovery, I've felt deep disconnection. I don't blame the porn industry for my past addiction. I chose to soothe my pain in that way and I eventually chose help. But, sadly, I have seen demeaning acts charading as sex.

As a citizen who cares about the disenfranchised and defenseless, I believe the pleasures of porn are not worth those wounded by it. The porn industry might deny its ties to sex-trafficking,[215] a trade that citizens heroically fight locally. Drug abuse, physical and psychological harm, and disease are commonplace;[216] sexuality and humanity are commodities.

These characteristics grate against my most essential beliefs in love, freedom, and human worth. I adamantly oppose those who profit from such atrocities. I once contributed to this industry through my addiction - an uncomfortable reality I must wrestle with.

Yes, I have a problem with the porn industry.

Maybe you do too. Maybe you'll avoid compensating porn's cause, telling businesses why you've withdrawn your support. Maybe you'll prepare picket signs, talk to city leaders, or use your influence in other ways. Standing together as a community, we can change Hustler's plans for our city.

Whatever form of *peaceful* opposition we're planning, let's consider another aspect of the opportunity before us. As we work to raise our community's standard, we can raise our personal standards as well. If we are caught by porn addiction, we can seek recovery. If our children are unprotected against porn, we can begin much-needed conversations and make necessary changes. We can take an active stance in the big battles behind our own doors. As we push porn out of all aspects of our lives, we can vote against the industry publicly without privately subsidizing its campaign.

Make no mistake, this is not a grievance against the goodness of sex. I love sex. I believe in people pursuing passionate, fun, and connected sex lives. But I believe this can only be achieved within a spirit of love. I have an anti-porn perspective because porn is anti-love.

If you believe in love, I invite you to express that through an active stance against the porn industry. Our stance spans our streets, our homes, and our hearts.

Will you vote for love? Your vote matters.

CHAPTER 31

———◆———

What One Person Can Do to Stand Against "Shades of Grey" [217]

Mission to Accomplish #6: Finding the courage to stand for my deepest convictions

Mission to Accomplish #7: Standing against objectification and sexual exploitation

Mission to Accomplish #8: Actively working to raise my community's standards regarding all forms of pornography

---

When I learned of Hollywood's plan to release the movie Fifty Shades of Grey in 2015, I was strongly compelled to write the following piece in opposition to the film.

As a therapist who specializes in sexual addiction treatment, I am deeply concerned about the release of the book-made-movie *Fifty Shades of Grey* this Valentine's Day weekend.

Not only does the *Fifty Shades* series portray pornographic and dehumanizing themes, it also glorifies highly abusive relational dysfunction. It is my hope to inspire citizens to stand against this movie in practical, meaningful ways.

Like other forms of pornography, this movie communicates messages of degradation, objectification and abuse. History's famed atrocities, from the slave trade to sex-trafficking, have been fueled by the objectification and dehumanization of people. These messages hurt all of us, especially the most innocent among us: our children.

A study published in the Journal of Women's Health [218] examined themes in the book with the help of abuse and sexual-practice experts. The results revealed extensive instances of emotional abuse, sexual violence, and reactions by the victim, Anastasia, that are typical of abused women. It was concluded that "pervasive intimate-partner violence" was a significant pattern.

This tale of romanticized violence is far from a love story. It is abuse-themed pornography, repackaged and glorified.

Action is essential. We must do something.

A Guide to What One Person Can Do About Pornography [219] instructs citizens on how to challenge and change their community standards regarding pornography. What prevents this essential change? Silence. "The only thing necessary for the triumph of evil is for good people to do nothing," [220] said Edmund Burke. We must speak up.

What can be done?

If you oppose the pornographic content and abusive attitudes of *Fifty Shades*, consider the following options:

1. **Let your money talk.** The more funds we withhold from theaters showing this movie, the clearer the message. If enough concerned citizens refuse to attend any movie in any theater showing it, we will send a strong message of protest. This can make a noticeable difference in profits.

2. **Put it in writing.** Theater managers who receive letters detailing why we are refraining from giving them business can more clearly assess if showing *Fifty Shades* is worth it, both financially and ethically. See *Appendix B* for a sample letter to send to local theaters.

3. **Invest in good.** Instead of paying to watch domestic violence on the silver screen, give your ticket money to support domestic violence shelters. If your past included frequenting massage parlors or prostitutes, consider sponsoring anti-trafficking organizations. Rather than personally pursuing porn, think about donating your resources to non-profits that promote pornography awareness or help people heal. These acts could even be a part of making amends for those recovering from an addiction that once strengthened the sexual objectification industry.

4. **Spread the word.** Engage in any opportunities you discover to tell others about the destructive nature of all forms of sexual exploitation. If news of this movement

moves your heart, please recommend *Life After Lust* to those in your influence.

5. **Join the movement.** Support change by joining the anti-pornography movement, partnering with organizations like The National Center on Sexual Exploitation and Fight the New Drug. I have also created *The Anti-Pornography Movement* [221] Facebook group for those seeking to stay in the loop and share resources.

6. **Persist and believe.** We can count on the porn industry and Hollywood to push the limits of what we will tolerate in our communities, including making more movies in the *Fifty Shades* series. Perseverance with our message is necessary and there are many success stories of people fighting pornography. This is a winnable war.

We have a profound opportunity. As Brennan Manning penned, "It is a courageous determination to make unpopular decisions that are expressive of the truth of who we are."[222] This is about adding action to our awareness. For anyone who believes in standing against the proliferation of pornography and sexual exploitation, this is a call to living a congruent life.

I beg you, please do not react to this film in a manner that contributes to the problem. We must speak out with dignity and respect. If you're a victim of abuse or in recovery, you're not disqualified from joining this cause. Often the wounded make the mightiest warriors. Your story fuels your fervency.

When we stand for what we believe in, change will happen. If not in the form of social transformation, it will undeniably happen in each of us as we let ourselves be seen. In the words of

Brené Brown, "The willingness to show up changes us, it makes us a little braver each time."[223]

Let's stand together courageously against *Fifty Shades of Grey* and other forms of pornography that engulf and entrap our world. Let's model to our children how to act boldly in the face of injustice. Let's do our part to challenge deteriorating community standards, creating safer societies for us all. May we live with integrity, spreading messages of healthy sexuality, authentic connection, and the worth of all people.

The following generations will thank us.

CHAPTER 32

◆━━━━◆

The Ripple Effects of Living in Alignment[224]

__Mission to Accomplish #9__: Learning to live in alignment with my values

---

We all experience moments when one choice changes the trajectory of our lives. For me, such an event occurred on February 6th, 2015. On that pivotal day, I posted the controversial piece *What One Person Can Do To Stand Against "Shades of Grey."*

As I prepared for my bold stance, I gleaned from Brennan Manning's wisdom regarding those who stand up for what they believe in. He wrote about how we can let go of other's opinions, as we connect more deeply with ourself.[225]

Manning's timely words resonated deeply with me. Beyond any moment in my personal history, writing *that* piece was standing strongly on my own two feet, proclaiming the truth that stirred within my heart.[226] Even if nobody stood with me, there was deep satisfaction in knowing that I did what I knew was right.

To say that it had a ripple effect would be understating the impact. When I shared this article with the world, it made waves...*huge* waves. The article views increased exponentially, arriving at 3625 on the 6th day alone, with thousands of shares. It received both praise and criticism. To date, the article has received almost 18,000 views and 5,500 shares on Facebook. This was the starting line of an amazing and unexpected season, brimming with opportunities to write, speak, teach, and connect with others. I did not know where my writing would lead me. I just knew what I needed to do and I did it.

Of greater value than the opportunities this action opened up was the character created in me. This was a journey of hope, trust, and courage. It expanded my perspective of what was possible. I am stronger, bolder, and more purpose-driven as a result. I wouldn't trade those internal results for anything. Even if the outward results were disastrous, it would've been worth the experience of inward alignment.

As we grow in our recovery, we learn who we are and we gain the courage to live that out. No longer are we bound by secrecy, constantly trying to cover up choices that cause us shame. In recovery, we learn to live with integrity. We are the same person in the dark that we are in the light. When our actions do not align with our values, our internal alarm system sounds. Tony Litster talks about it this way:

When I get off of the principles, I start to have friction in my life. I start to have discomfort. I start to have pain. To the level that I get out of alignment with the natural law, I experience discomfort and eventually, dis-ease...This is nature telling me "get back in alignment, dude! Get things back together."[227]

The concept of alignment is essential when we consider long-term recovery. When we become more of who we are, we will experience more discomfort when we revert to old actions. In his book *If You Know Who You Are You Will Know What to Do*, Greer explains, "No matter the reason or how inadvertent the error of my actions, if I know who I am and what I believe and *do not act* accordingly, I feel a sickening emptiness. And I hope I always will. For the pain pushes me to change and reminds me of the need for new maturity, depth, and awareness."[228]

The more we live in alignment, the greater our inner peace. Yes, we will also make more significant splashes in the world as we act honorably. But the greatest mountains will be moved inside of us, which is where we will discover the deepest meaning.

As you consider the concept of alignment, I urge you to answer the following questions:

1. What are your deepest values?
2. In what ways has your sexual addiction hindered your ability to live in alignment with those values?
3. Are there other negative habits that hamper your experience of alignment?
4. In what areas do you feel the most and least aligned? (Physical health, spirituality, family connection, marriage, friendships, stress management, etc.)

5. What bold steps have you taken to live aligned with who you are?

6. How could letting go of lust and learning to love contribute to your care for yourself and others?

7. What structural changes could you implement in your life that would strengthen your daily commitment to inner alignment?

    Starting or joining a group?

    Seeking out daily inspiration?

    Surrounding yourself with like-minded people?

    Stating your mission commitments daily?

    Searching out retreats that deepen self-care and growth?

8. What courageous leap lies ahead for you?

    The pursuit of a dream?

    The battle against an injustice?

    The initiative toward an ambitious goal?

    The commitment to recover from past wounds?

    The aim to deepen daily connection with those in your influence and care?

I am convinced that when we boldly live in alignment with our values, we experience possibilities that both blow our minds and expand our hearts. We give the world our greatest gifts. We repurpose passion for the greater good.

We cannot predict the outcomes of our actions but our lives are deeply enriched when we stand up, speak up, and become the change we want to see in the world.[229]

What can one person do?

You decide.

CHAPTER 33

Dear Porn:
A Father's Letter

Mission to Accomplish #10: Maintaining a connected relationship with my children

Mission to Accomplish #11: Proactively protecting my children from the threats of pornography

Mission to Accomplish #12: Proactively protecting the younger generation from the threats of pornography

This piece was originally published on the Protect Young Minds[230] (formerly Porn-Proof Kids) blog on Father's Day of 2015. While aimed at fathers, this important message applies to all parents.

Dear Porn,

I recall the first night we met. I was just a boy. Like the famed Piper, you played your tempting tune, and I danced blindly behind you, down your long, destructive path. For years my heart pledged allegiance to your ways. Each experience of escape only postponed my pain. I sank deep in shame.

Porn, how you must have mourned the day I closed my mind to your mantra, signing over my life to a higher calling. I sought strength in numbers, experiencing the reality of recovery. For the first time in a decade, you and I parted ways.

I look back on years of both challenge and triumph. No longer does your siren song echo in my ears.

Porn, our paths would cross again. Next time for nobler reasons.

I peer up to the horizon and see you creeping forward. Like a wolf longing for lambs, your eyes descend on my little ones. I see you salivating at the thought of one young life lost to lust. As you calculate your move on my children, do not forget the force of an infuriated father.

Still, you start your assault.

Like a poisonous fog, you sweep silently among the vulnerable, infecting the world's children in record numbers. Many remain unaware of your insidious influence.

May we rouse to the reality of your attack before we wake to the devastation of an addicted generation. You are in hot pursuit of our youngest members and we cannot stand idly by watching the carnage.

Porn, too often your efforts are effective. Stories abound of those caught in your tempting trance. Faithful to your reputation, you always strike; your wounded victims left for dead. Cunning and crafty, you convince countless to exchange long-term intimacy for immediate intensity. I ask:

- How many relationships have you ruined?
- How many marriages have you mauled?
- How many have deserted their purposeful path in pursuit of your mirage of pleasures?
- How many have chased your promises of passion, arriving at the dead-ends of disconnection and depression?

Incalculable numbers.

Such is life after porn. Our sons and daughters deserve better.

As you yearn for my young ones, I decisively declare that I will protect them.

As their father, I will wage war against you and your wicked ways.

As their father, I will expose you as my children's enemy. I will reveal to them who you are and how you can harm them, from their brains to their beliefs. I will point out where you lurk. I will equip them to evade you.

As their father, I will be my children's teacher. I will instruct them about the beauty of their bodies and the wonder of connected sexuality. I will contrast these great gifts to the cheap, corrupted counterfeits you offer them.

As their father, I will porn-proof my children's home and their hearts. Putting safeguards into place, I will protect their innocence, limiting easy and accidental access to you.

As their father, I will model what I expect of them. Striving to stand strong, I will seek forgiveness in the face of my mistakes.

I will care for myself in moments of pain, seeking connection over addiction. I will nurture my spiritual self, pursuing depth and dependence in that responsive relationship.

As their father, I will plant in my children deep roots of connection. My hands will hold their hearts when they are scared and sorrowful. Creating an atmosphere of safety and security, I will respond compassionately to their struggles and shortcomings. Lavished in love, ours will be a home of hugs and honesty. I will embrace them in their weaknesses, believing that when you tempt them, they will turn to me.

As their father, I acknowledge my imperfections as a parent. I choose to intentionally turn from a state of complacency to commitment.

Porn, today I am acutely aware of your dangerous dance and I am joined by thousands of fathers ready to call your bluff. Most of us recovering rebels, we are turning a deaf ear to your once mesmerizing music. We now know it as the sound of suffering.

As we observe the children gathering at your gate, we are sounding the alarm, alerting others of your impending attack. When you skillfully strike, your efforts will be met with mobs of resistance. We are at the front lines, ready to fight.

Abandoning passivity,[231] we battle for those living now and those yet to be born. We fight, not only for our own, but for those whose fathers are unavailable, unaware, or unwilling to join our unyielding ranks. The greatest gift we can deliver down to them is a legacy of love and freedom. As we charge forward on behalf of all sons and daughters, they will feel the infinite value you tried to tarnish.

For us, Father's Day carries profound meaning. It marks a moment in our year when we reveal to the world the worth of our families and the courageous measures we will take to protect them.

Porn, as we passionately oppose you today, it is not for misguided motivations. Our opposition flows from hearts of devotion, because this is what it means to be fathers.

CHAPTER 34

＊———◆———＊

The Wake-Up Call

Mission to Accomplish #13: Waking up and taking action when my recovery commitments begin to wane

Mission to Accomplish #14: Maintaining long-term recovery

Mission to Accomplish #15: Creating a legacy for future generations

---

One fateful day, I found myself living far out of alignment. Over a week into a family vacation to a Costa Rican paradise, I was caught in a descending spiral of disconnection and indulgence. Secretly scanning for scantily clad women while sporting my *I Love My Wife* T-shirt, I was active in a Jekyll-and-Hyde-like hypocrisy. I knew better. This, my first book, *Life After Lust,* was near completion: a resource aimed at unanchoring others from the destination I was drifting toward. I preached how vacations were never a respite from recovery, yet I was chasing sugar highs and indulging unrestrained eyes. Unbeknownst to me, this lust binge would end unexpectedly. A wake-up call was headed my way.

That evening, I walked with my family down to the beach to watch the sunset and play in the waves. Acutely aware of the female figures in my midst, I went out into the water with my kids, my wife watching from dry land. As the breakers hit my back, it briefly occurred to me that I should remove my glasses. I ignored the impulse. When the next wave crashed over me, I emerged to a blurred landscape. My glasses were gone.

I stood stunned by the gravity of the situation. I yelled out to my wife, sharing what had happened, knowing that the chances were slim that I would savor another sunrise on this once-in-a-lifetime trip. Like a child caught misbehaving, I felt this fate was deserved. Was this God's punishment for my out-of-control eyes? If so, it felt justified.

Faced with odds against my favor, I begged God for another chance. I vowed to Him that if I found my glasses, my eyes would be committed to fighting lust for the rest of the trip. Then I went to work. Under darkening skies, I began wading through the water, sifting through the sand with my toes, looking for my glasses. I repeatedly reached down, searching through the surging surf, bringing up handfuls of nothing. Using half-blind eyes to comb the wet landscape, I struggled against hopelessness, praying for a miracle.

Twenty minutes later my wife yelled out to me, hinting that it was time to go. Knowing my glasses could be anywhere in that bay by then, I held out hope, requesting five more minutes. I prayed one last time, then searched one last time. Seconds after I mentally murmured the petition "Lord," I looked down through the foamy waters. In eye-widening astonishment, I spotted below me the dark frames of my glasses. I instantly grabbed them, overcome with shock, relief, and gratitude. I placed my glasses on my wet face, turned toward the open ocean, closed my eyes, and savored the moment. I was overtaken by amazement, acknowledging the beauty of this blessing, this unearned gift. It was a profoundly spiritual experience.

Rising out of the water that night was like a second baptism. I walked out a different person. My resolve to fight lust, fueled by awe, was amplified to an all-time high. My recovery commitment was a solid ten.

My family was also surprised by my discovery. As we went back to our hotel room, we walked through the same setting with the same women present I had previously objectified. But this time, my motives were renewed. I refused to return to those self-destructive rituals.

I thought about the words I'd written in this book about us humbling ourselves before life humbles us, wondering if I'd bought the lie that I was the exception. Life had humbled me. In that mindset, I was ready to do what was necessary to achieve active recovery.

Planning for Success

My commitment to God was to live lust-free the rest of the trip. Knowing my environment was not going to change, I knew I had to change. Perched on the porch of my hotel room, I took pen to paper, writing out what I needed to do to fight for my freedom. I asked myself, "What needs to happen to throw my Evil Genius under the bus?" Intending to keep my recovery commitment level high, I created the following plan:

- Reconnect with my accountability partners.
- Attend an online recovery meeting.
- Abstain from alcohol.
- Abstain from sugar (since moderation wasn't working).
- Pray daily.
- Read the *Lie of Lust* and *Evil Genius* chapters of my book.
- Commit to my wife to not turn on the TV without her with me.
- Exercise daily.
- Take off my glasses when I'm near the pool.
- Practice mindful breathing ten minutes per day.
- Fight lust at a level ten.
- Focus on making great memories and connecting with my family.
- Communicate my new intentions to my accountability partners.

That night, I sent out an email to the men who hold me accountable, sharing about my wake-up call in the waves and my plan to exit attitudes of lethargy and lust. I later requested their confrontation if I, at a future date, were to sink back into lazy recovery. Looking back, I could see that slacking in my recovery work predated my vacation. Caught in a cycle of achievement seeking and stress, I too naturally neglected my needs.

When I went to bed I apologized to my wife saying, "I'm sorry for not working my recovery well on this trip. I will get back on track." Thankfully, she responded graciously. My apology was humbling, yet necessary, a much-needed reminder that my recovery was not just about me.

Action Means Everything

The next day I was back in action. Up before my family, I re-engaged my self-care routine. Following through with one commitment, I Skype-called into a *Sexaholics Anonymous* phone meeting. That misty morning, I stood under a beach umbrella by the pool, attempting to shield myself from the rain as I reconnected with others in recovery. My willingness to make that call showed *me* that I was serious. And I was. The effect from the previous evening's wake-up call cemented in me a strengthened commitment. I could not return to irresponsible recovery.

Through the remainder of my trip, I practiced much of what I planned, ending the vacation victorious over lust, just as I had set out to do. The trip was not without trials and temptations, but working my recovery and staying connected helped me steer clear of potential pitfalls. Even more importantly, I enjoyed moments with my family on our out-of-country adventure that I may have previously missed in my mindless daze. I wouldn't trade those memories we made together for anything.

When I returned from Costa Rica, I maintained my momentum, remaining actively engaged in my recovery. Since then, I've thought about the priceless experiences that would have evaded me had I stayed on the auto-pilot of my addiction: A soul-warming walk with God in our garden one cold, foggy morning. Clearing time to court my wife. An impromptu soccer game, just me and my boys. Reconnecting with my body and re-engaging in caring for it. Sharing the story of my wake-up call with friends and clients, watching the ripple effect of their ramped up resolve. Catching the fresh scent of a mission more massive than me. Living in the light of a transparent life. Responding to temptations with the reminder that my glasses were a gift. These experiences were given to me in active recovery and I am sincerely grateful I was shocked back into the battle for life after lust.

The Pitfalls and Possibilities of Long-Term Recovery

This story could stir up in you a variety of responses. Maybe you're feeling disillusioned, wondering how someone with over a decade of sobriety could slip back into lustful living. Maybe you're questioning, "What's the big deal," wondering why my state of stagnation was so significant. Maybe you see yourself in these scenarios, feeling abruptly awakened from your own daze of denial. Regardless of how this story sits in your mind's eye, here's one glaring truth I hope you'll get from it: There are both potential pitfalls and purposeful possibilities in long-term recovery. Here are some pitfalls you may encounter in long-term recovery:

- Giving in to the lure of laziness with essential recovery habits.
- Letting the search for significance lead to significant stress.
- Avoiding sexual acting out yet numbing in new ways.
- Wandering into a lukewarm attitude toward visual and fantasy lust and objectification, thinking "at least I'm not doing what I used to do."
- Judging healthy pleasures like play, relaxation, and connected sex as unproductive, cutting them from your calendar.
- Thinking you've arrived, when recovery won't end till you take your last breath.
- Striving and settling for attention over connection.

- Loosening boundaries with people, time, and tempting situations.
- Believing recovery can be done alone, even though it took a community to get you here.
- Distracting yourself from Divine connection.
- Loving productivity over people.
- Putting too much stock in your sobriety date as the only sign of your growth and worth.
- Getting too busy to notice the rain, your pain, and those calling your name.
- Failing to face the wounds of your past and present, once they're no longer numbed out.
- Falling into perfectionistic, hateful, and shame-based beliefs about yourself, your body, and your behavior.
- Quitting too easily in the face of failures, difficulties, or when struggles seem to go away.
- Comparing yourself to others, believing you'll never measure up.[232]
- Blaming everything and everyone for your choices to live out of alignment.
- Serving others so much that you abandon personal needs and wants.[233]
- Prioritizing destiny over legacy.[234]

The purposeful possibilities of long-term recovery are endless and unique to each person. They could include:

- Spiritual transformation and deepened intimacy with the Divine.
- Motives no longer powered by pain, shame, and secrets.

- Finding and fostering connection with loved ones.
- The prospect of a heart that is healing.
- Experiencing the fulness of life, once finally reconnected to feelings.[235]
- Discovering the value of others, ceasing to see them as sex objects or as people to be used.
- Moving from fantasy into reality.
- No longer neglecting needs but learning to love yourself.
- Discovering your true self.[236]
- Finding freedom and passing that hope to others.
- Pursuing a new career, calling, or mission.
- Joining the human community: "claiming your seat in the world."[237]
- Living an intentional, engaged life.[238]
- Knowing your worth, deep down in your soul.
- Coming alive, like never before.

As you can see, recovery is a journey packed with many potential pitfalls and possibilities. I believe the more prepared we are for the pitfalls, the more engaged we'll be in the possibilities.

Sadly, the opposite is also true, the less effort we invest in avoiding the pitfalls, the less possibilities we'll experience in our lives.

Don't Waste Your Wake Up Call

Looking at the previous lists should make one thing clear: there's a lot at stake when it comes to your recovery. It is about far more than just losing or finding yourself (which is still significant). The results of staying asleep in recovery will affect many. This was the case for me when I woke up and sought treatment nearly thirteen years ago. It was also the case when I experienced my Costa Rican wake-up call. Having heeded my wake-up calls, I am progressively changing. I am far from flawless; my heart is still healing. Though I am not perfect, I am present. I am present with the people and passions that matter most to me and this makes all the difference. Frankly, had I remained asleep in addiction, many amazing things never would have materialized in my life, including this book. Nobody can predict the power of one person waking up from the auto-pilot of addiction and pursuing help.

If you find yourself fading in your recovery resolve, what do you think will be *your* wake-up call? Relapse? Tragedy? Unforeseen consequences? A near miss?[239] A miracle? My story? What surprising circumstance or shocking catastrophe will open your eyes to the wide open window of opportunity before you?

Some would call such an experience "hitting rock bottom." I have seen so many people wait for life's megaphone of misery before they're willing to look at themselves and seriously consider change. It's not a pretty sight and they wouldn't wish it on anyone, but the lessons learned from those experiences are like gold refined by fire.

Though your wake up call may come through crisis, it is packed with possibility. Pain is a powerful teacher. When awakened by the pain of reckless living, I urge you to do something different. Don't doze back to sleep. Let your alarm lead to action. Make a plan. Recruit a team. Set up a system that supports sleeplessness on the road of recovery. Remember, if you wake-up, you are still alive and there's more life to live. Engage in your life. We need you back in the game.

Don't waste your wake-up call.

A Life Worth Waking Up For

Of course, there are downsides to waiting for your wake-up call. One is that you can't predict what consequences will come along with it. It seems our imaginations are weak when we consider where our addiction will take us. Another significant downside to this strategy is that nobody is promised a wake-up call. The truth is, it may never come. Or when it comes, you may not want to hear it, turning a deaf ear. With this in mind, the choice is yours: You can passively wait for your unpredictable wake-up call while life passes you by or you can take heed and take action right now. Should you choose to accept it, *this is your wake up call*.

There is no time like the present to begin again. Take a look at your life. In what ways are you asleep at the wheel? How have you drifted away from active recovery, toward the potential pitfalls shared previously? Consider the beforementioned possibilities of long-term recovery. Which one resonates the most with you? Which one is most worth waking up for? Will you choose to wake up now?

Even for the most depressed among us, I believe there is a life worth waking up for. There are so many worthwhile reasons to wake up and pursue passionate recovery. Still, I know from experience that the first steps are the heaviest. In despair, you may look at your life and wonder how you'll move beyond where you are now. You may size yourself up, believing that with your shameful history, you're not worth the effort. It may seem impossible to muster the awareness to wake from the comfortable sleep you're caught in. But if you don't wake up, you'll miss so much. And we'll miss so much of *you*. Tony Litster echoes this encouragement:

You have such a gift to offer. There's only one of you. You have this unique background, this unique experience, this unique history, perspective, and unique gifts and talents that are only yours and there will only be one of you. Part of this game we play together on planet earth is, as we wake-up, we help other people wake-up. Because I rely on you sharing your gifts and living your purpose as much as you rely on me living mine. We're here to remind each other of that. So start to wake-up.[240]

Believe it or not, out of your healing will come your gifts to the world. I have found this to be true in my own life. I have witnessed this in the lives of clients and friends. Those who have battled their way to freedom are among my greatest heroes. Watching others wake-up and engage in their lives is one of the most rewarding things I've witnessed in life.

Living a Legacy

A sure sign of recovery is the transition from being singularly self-focused to caring about the world as well. As we grow, we become less *me* focused and more *we* focused.[241] When healing happens, we see the impact on those in our midst. As we strive to stay awake in recovery, may we learn how to live out a legacy that outlasts us. In the words of Erwin McManus, "Living wide awake is about realizing that the world needs [us] to live up to [our] potential."[242] Our decision to engage in recovery affects others in ways we'll never fully know.

Recovering from lust addiction, we gain new eyes that see beyond our egos into a future where everyone matters. With awakened eyes, we will see that living without lust is just the beginning. Learning to let go of lust, we can connect with the mission to move beyond our destiny, creating a legacy of love for generations to come.

And that, my friends, is worth waking up for.

Conclusion

To The One Shackled by Sexual Addiction,
I wish one thing for you: freedom.

Both freedom *from* and freedom *to*.

I wish for you freedom *from* shame and self-imposed suffering. Freedom *from* debilitating secret-driven fears. Freedom *from* self-hatred and self-neglect. Freedom *from* punishment and pain. Freedom *from* the auto-pilot of addiction.

I wish for you freedom *to* heal and *to* feel. Freedom *to* lavishly love others. Freedom *to* fight for yourself and the ones you cherish most. Freedom *to* generously give back. Freedom *to* champion worthy causes. Freedom *to* live.

Lasting freedom.

As you've read the preceding pages, maybe you've realized that recovery from sexual addiction is bigger than you. I mean this in two ways. First, sexual addiction is a strong force to reckon with, requiring *mindsets* of responsibility, consistency, and courage. Recovery is actualized through the progressive advancement from Novice to *Master*.

Second, your recovery affects the rest of humanity. Healing begins in you, then reaches your relationships, then ripples into the world. The powers that propel pornography and the sex industry gain opposition with each person free from their grip. In recovery, you connect with your meaningful *mission* and this impacts everyone.

Sexual addiction is bigger than you but I believe you will beat it. I urge you to sense the urgency. There is no time like the present to use the knowledge found in this book to initiate the dawn of your new day.

Use this information as both motivation and inspiration. Dr. Wayne Dyer differentiates between the two by writing that motivation is when you grab hold of an idea and inspiration is when an idea grabs hold of you.[243]

Will you catch the scent of an *inspired* recovery? Will you allow the potential to permeate deep into your soul?

I sincerely hope you will. I invite you onto the well-worn path of those who have battled before you. It is time to rise up and live the life you are meant to live.

It is time to rise up and live out life after lust.

Your Recovery Roadmap:
A 52-Week Plan

Every *Essential Mindset, Skill to Master,* and *Mission to Accomplish* presented in this book is important for successful recovery. Thus, I have created *Your Recovery Roadmap: A 52-Week Plan*, providing a recommended structure for learning and practicing the concepts of *Life After Lust*. Ideally, this plan should be used in conjunction with a recovery or treatment program, led by a trained sexual addiction specialist, whenever possible. In order to complete this one year plan you will need the book *Life After Lust,* a private recovery journal, and a commitment to persevere through the process. This *52-Week Plan* can be a life-changing experience, should you *choose* to make it so.

It should be noted that the resources recommended in this *Recovery Roadmap* are from varying perspectives. This can be helpful to see the range of resources available for those seeking help. Since each person pursuing recovery has a unique background, I cannot tell you which resources will fit your specific situation. Each resource in this section should be researched by the individual to determine the best fit for personal circumstances and alignment with each person's values and beliefs. This is in no way an all-inclusive list; there are many other excellent resources available that are not provided here.

The following is a recommended *52-Week Plan* for those ready to work their way to life after lust:

Week 1:
Life After Lust Reading:

Introduction

Assignment: Get a journal and write down your feelings and thoughts about what you read. Will you join me on the path of passionate recovery?

Skill to Master #2: Humbly reaching for help

Assignment: Reach out to a sexual addiction therapist and/or program. The recovery journey begins with finding the right help and reaching out for it. It is highly recommended that anyone engaging in sexual behavior that feels out of control, compulsive, or results in the harm of self or others consult a certified sexual addiction therapist who can test for the presence of a sexual addiction and provide treatment. You can take the online Sexual Addiction Screening Test (at www.recoveryzone .com/tests/sex-addiction/SAST/index.php) but an in person assessment is preferred, when possible. Professional help will likely be necessary for treating disorders that co-occur with the addiction, such as depression, anxiety, and ADHD. Getting treatment for past trauma is also important. Long-term sobriety will remain elusive if these underlying issues are not treated.

To find a sexual addiction therapist near you, look for the following certifications:

Sexual Addiction Treatment Provider (SATP)

Certified Sex Addiction Therapist (CSAT)
https://www.iitap.com/resources

American Association for Sex Addiction Therapy
https://aasat.org/find-therapist

My highest recommendation would be to find a therapist with one of the above certifications who works within the structure of a sexual addiction treatment program such as LifeSTAR and offers a therapeutic recovery group. Another benefit of LifeSTAR is they provide a program for traumatized partners and some affiliates have YouthSTAR programs for addicted adolescents as well. To find a LifeSTAR program near you, check out the LifeSTAR Network map at www.lifestarnetwork.com/the-solution/get-help-now.

I recommend asking the following questions before beginning sexual addiction treatment with a therapist:[244]

1. *What training or certification do you have for treating sexual addiction?* Do some personal research based on their answer.
2. *Do you work from an attachment-based model in treating addictions?*"Yes" is the most helpful answer.
3. *Do you provide therapeutic recovery groups?* If not, you will need a community-based or online recovery group to supplement any individual or couples therapy done with this therapist.

4. *Do you offer help for traumatized partners (if needed)?* If so, what is your approach in helping partners of sex addicts? A trauma perspective is necessary.

5. *How many sexually addicted clients have you treated?* Hopefully, many.

6. *Are you trained to facilitate a formal Disclosure?* If not, you can still work with them but it is suggested that you find someone else to facilitate the Disclosure.

7. *Do you do couples therapy? If so, how do you work with them?* Learning to rebuild trust and connect will be primary pieces of couples work. Couples work will be most helpful if both individuals are actively working their recovery.

8. *Are you familiar with the 12-Steps?* This will be helpful if you plan to do a 12-Step based program.

Many sexual addiction ministries are also available, such as:

- New Creation Ministries - http://ncmfresno.org
- Transformed Hearts - http://transformedhearts.com

Inpatient or intensive treatment may also be warranted depending on the severity of your situation. Here are some possibilities:

- LifeSTAR Intensive Outpatient
  www.lifestarnetwork.com/the-solution/iop/
- Faithful & True - www.faithfulandtrue.com
- Bethesda (for female addicts as well)
  www.bethesdaworkshops.org

- The Meadows - www.themeadows.com/
  conditions-we-treat/sexual-addiction
- Center for Healthy Sex - http://centerforhealthysex.com
- Heart to Heart Counseling Center
  http://sexaddict.com/sex-addiction-intensives/
- Integrity Redeemed Workshops
  www.integrityredeemed.com

Week 2:
Life After Lust Reading:

Dear Mr. Duggar: When Sexual Secrets Surface

Assignment: Write down the five recommendations presented in this chapter. Are you willing to commit to pursuing all of them? Which ones will be the hardest for you?

Essential Mindset #14: I deserve healing and wholeness.

Assignment: Write down and review this mindset daily this week.

Skill to Master #4: Working cooperatively with a sexual addiction therapist.

Assignment: Share this book with your therapist and explain the *52-Week Plan* to supplement therapy/treatment.

Week 3:

Life After Lust Reading:

Called to Rise

Assignment: Write down your answers to all questions presented in this chapter.

Essential Mindset #4: I will give up everything that hinders long-term recovery.

Assignment: Write down and review this mindset daily this week. What is hindering your long-term recovery (see chapter for examples)? Are you willing to exchange those things for the hope of recovery?

Essential Mindset #3: Sexual addiction is serious, requiring my immediate attention.

Assignment: Write down and review this mindset daily this week.

Week 4:

Life After Lust Reading:

Don't Be a Victim to Sexual Addiction

Essential Mindset #6: I take full responsibility for my past, present, and future choices.

Assignment: Write down and review this mindset daily this week.

Assignment: Write down your answers to these questions presented in this week's reading:

1. What choices led me into sexual addiction?
2. What choices can I make now?
3. If I believe there is always a way out of temptation, how hard will I look for it? To what lengths will I go to make sure I find it?
4. How am I acting helpless against pornography, lust, and other acting-out behaviors?
5. Do I *want* to change? If yes, am I *willing* to change? In other words, am I willing to do everything it takes to change?
6. In what ways am I making myself vulnerable to temptation?
7. What needs to change in my life to help me tap into my Higher Power's strength and the support of others?
8. What are my potential blind spots and what resources will help me see the truth in these areas (this may include asking others about your blindspots)?
9. What wounds have I ignored throughout my life that are in need of my attention?
10. What strengths, gifts, and abilities can I leverage in my recovery?
11. Who can I reach out to for help?
12. Will I take responsibility for my recovery?

Week 5:

Skill to Master #6: Protecting myself internally and externally

Assignment: Set up filtering or accountability software to limit easy access to pornography and other acting out behaviors. If you choose Covenant Eyes, please use the code **safepath.**

Assignment: Create boundaries for yourself, writing out what tempting situations you will avoid.

Week 6:

Life After Lust Reading:

The Paradox of Pornography Addiction: What You Fear Most Will Heal You

Essential Mindset #7: Permanent sobriety is always possible.

Assignment: Write down and review this mindset daily this week. In my experience, this mindset is essential, especially in the beginning. It helped me believe in and achieve long-term sobriety from compulsive pornography use. I have often heard the phrase "relapse is part of recovery." In my opinion, this phrase is only helpful after a relapse because it helps us learn from the experience. Looking ahead, we can do whatever is necessary to never relapse again.

Skill to Master #8: Learning to connect in the context of a recovery group

Assignment: Find a sexual addiction recovery group to attend at least once per week. This could be a therapeutic group (such as LifeSTAR - www.lifestarnetwork.com/the-solution/get-help-now) led by a sexual addiction specialist or a community based recovery group (like a 12-Step program). Recovery groups are available nationally (some internationally) such as:

- Celebrate Recovery (sexual purity groups)
- Sexaholics Anonymous
- Sex Addicts Anonymous

Online groups are available as well, such as:

- InTheRooms.com
- XXXChurch - http://x3groups.com
- Forest Benedict, LMFT, SATP - Online recovery groups/seminars available in the near future (hopefully).

Some groups also have phone meetings (such as Sexaholics Anonymous). While these meeting are helpful, in person groups are preferred.

Week 7:
Life After Lust Reading:

For the Christian Choosing Digital Adultery: Seven Strategies for Finding Freedom (People of all spiritual backgrounds will benefit from this article and assignment).

Assignment: Write down your answers to the following questions, based on this week's reading:

1. What are the three ways relationships are harmed by sexual addiction?
2. How has your addiction impacted others?
3. What other consequences have you experienced as a result of your addiction?
4. Are you willing to pursue all 7 crucial strategies for finding freedom presented in this chapter?
5. Which ones will be the most challenging for you?

Essential Mindset #11: Love is the antidote of lust; healing happens through connection.

Assignment: Write down and review this mindset daily this week.

Week 8:

Skill to Master #5: Learning to trust my Higher Power

Learning *to trust* a Higher Power is much different than learning *about* a Higher Power. Both are important in recovery. In recovery, learning to connect will be difficult for most, especially those with attachment difficulties. I have found that learning about *spiritual attachment* is an important part of this journey. You can find resources that fit your spiritual beliefs. I write about spiritual attachment on forestbenedict.com and have created the *Healing Through Connection Workbook* for my clients (Coming soon for public use), which explains attaching spiritually and in all other areas.

Here are some books I have found helpful:

Anatomy of the Soul: Surprising Connections Between Neuroscience and Spiritual Practices (Thompson, 2010)

God Attachment: Why You Believe, Act, and Feel the Way You Do About God (Straub & Clinton, 2010)

Emotionally Healthy Spirituality (Scazzero, 2006)

Abba's Child: The Cry of the Heart for Intimate Belonging (Manning, 1997)

Fathered by God: Learning What Your Dad Could Never Teach You (Eldredge, 2009)

Coming Clean (Levis, 2016)

Assignment: Find a book or resource that helps you grow in the area of spiritual attachment/connection. 2) Find a practice that strengthens spiritual connection and practice it daily, indefinitely. This practice may evolve over time. Learning to trust a Higher Power will be a lifelong journey.

Week 9:
Life After Lust Reading:

Introduction to Mindset section

Assignment: Print out the complete list of *Essential Mindsets* found at LifeAfterLust.com and place them where you will see them on a daily basis. Based on your understanding of recovery, what *Essential Mindsets* would you add to this list? Commit to memorizing this list over the next month. Find a book that inspires and strengthens your mindset for successful recovery.

Recommended Reading:

Wild at Heart: Discovering the Secret of a Man's Soul (Eldredge, 2001)

Week 10:
Life After Lust Reading:

Disclosure 101: The Art of Coming Clean

Assignment: Write down your answers to the following questions, based on this week's reading:

1. How have secrets fueled your addiction?
2. What forms of confession are you willing to implement in your life? Possibilities could include doing a formal Disclosure with a trained therapist, writing and sharing your Inventory with your group or sponsor, weekly accountability group sobriety check-in, agreement to disclose to partner if a relapse occurs, etc.
3. Are you willing to seek help and learn more about this topic so that you can make an informed decision on how to disclose past or future acting out behaviors?

Essential Mindset #18: Rather than doing as little as possible, I will do as much as   necessary to recover.

Assignment: Write down and review this mindset daily this week.

Skill to Master #7: Disclosing to my partner my acting out history with the help of a trained professional

Assignment: Schedule a session with a sexual addiction therapist to discuss the possibility of doing a formal Disclosure.

Week 11:
Life After Lust Reading:

What My Wife is Worth

Assignment: Print a copy of this week's reading (or a modified version based on your relationship) and post it somewhere where you can see it. Read it out loud daily. Print a copy of *What I Am Worth* (or a modified version based on your relationship) and give it to your partner as a reminder that they are worth fighting for (this part can be skipped if your therapist recommends against this based on your personal circumstance). See Appendix A. Downloadable files of both versions available at https://forestbenedict.com/2016/06/27/what-she-is-worth what-i-am-worth-new-downloadable-resources-for-daily-inspiration/

Essential Mindset #13: My partner is worth my best recovery efforts.

Assignment: What does it mean to do your *best* in recovery? How can you increase your commitment to your recovery (practically)? Remember, learning how to work a strong recovery will not happen overnight and will take much practice, patience, courage, and self-compassion.

Skill to Master #3: Caring for those wounded by my addiction.

Assignment: If you are in a committed relationship, encourage your partner to get help. Their level of care will depend on their level of trauma. They will likely need a program, therapy, and guidance/support for working their own recovery. There are many great resources available for partners. I've created a list of some resources here:

https://LifeSTARCentralValley.wordpress.com/partner-resources

Recommended Resource:

Building Unshakable Trust - http://eldridge-machen.my kajabi.com/store/BQ2FMjF3

Week 12:
Life After Lust Reading:

How Paying Attention Protects Our Children from Porn

Mission to Accomplish #11: Proactively protecting my children from the threats of pornography

Assignment: Set up filtering and accountability software to limit your children's easy access to pornography on all devices. Do your research on what program fits your family best. If you use Covenant Eyes, please use the code **safepath.**

Skill to Master #25: Learning to pay attention to my children, fostering deeper connection

Assignment: Review the four strategies for paying attention presented in this week's   chapter. Using a 1-10 scale, rate your effectiveness in each of these areas:

Pay attention to their access - Rating: _____

Pay attention to their habits - Rating: _____

Pay attention to their interests - Rating: _____

Pay attention to their emotions - Rating: _____

If shame is triggered during this exercise, practice self-compassion and commit to learning how to improve in each area.

Recommended Resources:

Good Pictures, Bad Pictures: Porn-Proofing Today's Young Kids (Jenson, 2014)

What's the Big Deal about Pornography?: A Guide for the Internet Generation (Manning, 2008) - for teenagers

Angry Birds and Killer Bees: Talking to Your Kids About Sex (Bowman, 2013)

Protect Young Minds - http://protectyoungminds.org

Mamacrossroads.com
Children, Teens, and Parents Resources -
https://lifestarcentralvalley.wordpress.com/children-teens-and-parents/

Pornography addiction resources for teenagers include YouthSTAR (www.lifestarnetwork.com/the-addiction/youthstar-2) and Fortify (https://fortifyprogram.org).

Week 13:

Life After Lust Reading:

The Lie of Lust

Essential Mindset #8: Lust is a lie and never satisfies

Assignment: Write down and review this mindset daily this week.

Essential Mindset #9: I will not objectify others, using them addictively.

Assignment: Write down and review this mindset daily this week.

Assignment: Honestly answer the questions presented in this week's reading:

1. Thinking about your personal history, how long have you depended on lust-filled living?
2. In what ways has lust diminished your quality of life?
3. How has lustful living deepened disconnections from your loved ones?
4. Do lust and objectification go against your highest values? Which ones?
5. Is the temporary lust-high worth the long-term losses that could result?
6. Despite its difficulty, are you willing to pursue the high calling of a lust-free life?

Week 14:
Life After Lust Reading:

Five Reasons to Fire Your Accountability Partner

Skill to Master #9: Learning to connect through a same-gender accountability relationship

Assignment: Considering the *red flags* of a weak accountability relationship; what would you guess are the characteristics of a strong accountability relationship? Find a same-gender accountability partner. The following is an excerpt from my *Healing Through Connection Workbook* (Benedict - Coming soon for public use), which explains accountability further:

An Accountability Partner is defined as someone who knows about your recovery commitments and whose job is to hold you to them. An Accountability Partner is different from a mentor or sponsor. It is recommended that they be someone who is on the same level as you, meaning they too are in recovery from sexual addiction and committed to that journey. This accountability relationship is a mutual commitment; you will be a resource for one another.

You may find a good Accountability Partner candidate in your group, at a 12-step meeting, or within a current friendship. Look for someone of the same gender who is committed to confidentiality, brutal honesty, and learning the grueling process of both achieving sobriety and connecting.

While you will have others in your support network, it is recommended that your Accountability Partner know everything

about your addiction history and your present progress. Otherwise, there may be a temptation to withhold information and tell only what you feel comfortable sharing with different people. This will also inform their questions because they will understand your triggers and see your blind-spots. Thus, complete honesty is necessary for complete healing.

Remember, you are not just in recovery from sexual addiction but also recovering from a life of lies, secrecy, and a shame-based identity. Attempting to control the circumstances by limiting vulnerability and protecting yourself from hurt or rejection will rob you of the experience of complete acceptance and love from another person. These patterns have kept you disconnected throughout your life and it's time to reconnect with safe people. Someone needs to see the full picture. Otherwise, they will not be able to understand and empathize with your experience and hold you accountable to your commitments.

For these reasons, it is recommended that you meet weekly, face-to-face, with your Accountability Partner and share with them all of the slips, struggles, and emotional pain you've experienced throughout the week. In his book The Game Plan (2005), Joe Dallas recommends setting up predetermined questions that your accountability partner will ask you, based on your specific struggles and weaknesses, ending with the question "Have you answered these questions honestly?"[245] As you create your questions, remember the underlying attachment-related purpose. All of the your questions are basically asking this: "Have you disconnected from what is unhealthy and connected with what is healthy this week?"[246]

Recommended Reading:

Healing Through Connection Workbook (Benedict - Coming soon for public use)

The 7 Principles of Highly Accountable Men (Laaser, 2011)

Week 15:
Life After Lust Reading:

Pursuing Peace When the World's at War

Skill to Master #19: Seeking and sustaining inner peace

Assignment: What experiences or activities provide you with a sense of inner peace? Add some of these to your daily, weekly, monthly, and yearly schedule.

Week 16:
Life After Lust Reading:

Escaping the Grip of Your Evil Genius

Essential Mindset #16: I will not engage in friendly conversation with my Evil Genius but will maintain an attitude of opposition, looking for ways to throw it under the bus.

Assignment: Using this chapter as a guide, write down the main tactics *your* Evil Genius uses to try to lure you back into your addiction. Create a plan to *throw your Evil Genius under the bus* that you can utilize in times of temptation.

Week 17:
Life After Lust Reading:

From Under the Rock

Essential Mindset #19: I will find my inspiration for recovery and connect with it daily.

Assignment: What strategies can you utilize to conjure up the necessary, daily inspiration for your recovery? Pick at least one inspiration ritual to practice on a daily basis, indefinitely.

Recommended Resource:

https://www.facebook.com/groups/InspirationCommunity

Week 18:

Skill to Master #31: Preparing for potential temptations

Assignment: When I was in early recovery I learned how to be vigilant in avoiding (whenever possible) situations that would trigger me to want to act out my addiction. I created boundaries for myself, such as avoiding video stores (back when there was such a thing) and not watching movies with nudity or sexual content. Looking back, I see the wisdom in these tactics and I believe they helped me achieve sobriety, especially in early recovery.

Now, when I hear that a recovering sex addict unexpectedly found themselves watching a movie with sexual content, I consider their experience the result of both poor planning and poor recovery work. These types of triggers are avoidable. As

Matt Fradd says, "It is the good warrior who is cognizant of [their] weak spots."[247]

This week, check out the site *PluggedIn.com* or find a similar resource where you can research the content of movies and other media before watching them. Maintaining commitments to avoid sexual content and triggering situations will benefit your recovery and the recovery of your partner as well. These commitments will evolve over time as you grow in your recovery. Initially, this may seem like a sacrifice but in the end it will be worth it; it will be one more step in doing whatever it takes.

Take a few minutes to think about all of your easy passageways into pornography use and other acting out behaviors (unmonitored computer/phone, alluring relationships, risky scenarios, etc) and be proactive, preparing now to protect yourself in the future. Set up a plan for each situation that presents a possible risk to your recovery.

Week 19:
Life After Lust Reading:

The Neuroscience of Self-Care

Skill to Master #10: Consistent and effective self-care

Assignment: Evaluate your current self-care routines (or lack thereof). After reading this chapter, write about the role of self-care in your recovery. What changes need to be made in this area? Based on this chapter, add some daily self-care habits to your schedule. Consider seeing a Doctor before making dietary, exercise, or lifestyle changes.

Essential Mindset #1: Recovery from sexual addiction is difficult, possible, and worth the effort.

Assignment: Write down and review this mindset daily this week.

Recommended Resource:

The Willpower Instinct: How Self-Control Works, Why It Matters, and What You Can Do to Get More of It (McGonigal, 2011)

Week 20:
Life After Lust Reading:

Permission to Rest

Skill to Master #11: Healthy self-soothing and relaxation

Assignment: Make a list of healthy self-soothing and relaxation activities that you enjoy (see *Running On Empty* for examples). Add some of these activities to your life, knowing that without them you are more vulnerable to relapse.

Week 21:
Life After Lust Reading:

Dealing with "Demons": Healing from a Shame-Based Identity

Skill to Master #12: Shame management

Assignment: After reading this week's chapter, do you believe you have a shame-based identity? In what ways are you committed to battling shame through inward and outward connection? This is one area where therapy (a form of outward connection) may be necessary, especially if some of your shame is rooted in trauma or abuse. Remember, shame management and learning to be self-compassionate are key components of recovery. Take a few minutes to test your level of self-compassion and write down your score:

http://self-compassion.org/test-how-self-compassionate-you-are

Week 22:
Life After Lust Reading:

The Courage of Self-Connection

Skill to Master #13: Self-connection

Skill to Master #16: Minimizing self-criticism

Skill to Master #14: Self-compassion

Assignment: One powerful tool I have recommended to clients for self-connection is called the Journaling Awareness Worksheet (Yerkovich). This resource can be found on HowWeLove.com (in *Freebies*). I suggest using this worksheet or another self-connection exercise regularly.

Assignment: Read or listen to a book about shame. I recommend one of the following:

1. *The Neuroscience of Change: A Compassion-Based Program for Personal Transformation*, Dr. Kelly McGonigal (2012)
2. *Daring Greatly: How the Courage to Be Vulnerable Transforms the Way We Live, Love, Parent, and Lead* (Brené Brown, 2015)
3. *The Soul of Shame: Retelling the Stories We Believe About Ourselves* (Thompson, 2015)

Week 23:
Life After Lust Reading:

Recovering from Relapse

Skill to Master #17: Self-forgiveness

Skill to Master #18: Rising quickly from perceived failures

Assignment: Practice the *Failure Response Worksheet* presented in this week's reading. Commit to implementing this tool after perceived failures in maintaining recovery routines and sobriety. Are you willing to forgive yourself for past mistakes, recommit, and get back on the road of recovery?

Week 24:

Skill to Master #15: Emotional regulation (managing pain and emotion)

Essential Mindset #15: I will grow in self-love, responding with care when I experience emotional pain.

Assignment: Write down your answers to the following questions:

1. How do you respond to your emotions? Are self-neglect, self-directed anger, and self-abandonment your self-defeating normal responses?

2. Are you committed to learning how to relate to yourself in a loving, caring, and self-compassionate way, even though this will feel foreign and undeserved? For most of us, this will be a new realm of learning. Take 30 minutes this week to explore http://self-compassion.org. Commit to adding a self-compassion exercise to your daily routine so that you can master this necessary recovery skill.

Assignment: While emotional regulation skills are important, those who have more intense emotional experiences, such as victims of abuse or other trauma and those suffering from depression, anxiety, and other mental health challenges, should seek professional help (individual therapy). Sometimes medication and other forms of treatment are necessary and will make a significant difference for those pursuing recovery. Another significant skill for managing emotion is learning how to reach out to relationships or emotional support. Often, learning how to do this will begin in therapy. If you struggle in any of the above areas, seek out the professional support you need.

Week 25:

Skill to Master #29: Learning to have fun apart from addiction

Assignment: Fun is an essential part of life, yet something many addicts have difficulty practicing.[248] Addicts "demonstrate an almost complete inability to relax and enjoy themselves,"[249] so learning how to have fun without your drugs of choice is a significant challenge of recovery. In successful long-term recovery, learning how to have fun is non-negotiable. Read the article called *Are We Having Fun Yet?* (https://lifestarcentralvalley. wordpress.com/2014/09/06/are-we-having-fun-yet) and write down one activity you could regularly implement into your life from each of the categories presented (recreation, enjoying nature, family fun, music, etc). Based on your list, try one this week. Again, choose something that is not addictive (consuming excessive sugar, gambling, pornography, etc). Video games are not recommended for this exercise due to their affect on the brain you are working hard to heal.[250]

Week 26:
Life After Lust Reading:

My Path Out of Porn Addiction: A Therapist's Journey

Essential Mindset #2: Past pain that made me vulnerable to addiction must be addressed for healing to occur.

Assignment: Often sex addicts have emotional pain that contributes significantly to their addiction. Many have trauma and most have been emotionally neglected in their early life. Go to the website http://www.drjonicewebb.com and take the Emotional Neglect Questionnaire to assess the level of emotional neglect in your childhood. If your score is high, I recommend you buy Dr Webb's book *Running On Empty: Overcome Your Childhood Emotional Neglect* to begin your healing journey in this area. For all types of abuse or neglect, I strongly recommend therapy. Quality sexual addiction treatment programs will also treat trauma. Community programs such as *Adult Children of Alcoholics/Dysfunctional Families* may also be helpful, depending on your background. Healing from trauma and emotional pain will be a long-term process.

Week 27:
Life After Lust Reading:

Defending Against Prelapse: From Passivity to Passion

Essential Mindset #17: I will maintain my recovery momentum by actively opposing passivity and fueling my passion.

Assignment: After reading this week's chapter, write down your answers to the following questions regarding your recovery:

- In what ways am I passive, in a state of *prelapse?*
- How is denial adding to my lack of passion in my recovery?
- Have I become lazy in practicing necessary self-care for maintaining my recovery?
- What am I doing well in my recovery?

- Am I practicing patterns of disconnection in my relationships with my Higher Power, myself, and with my support network?
- In what ways am I walking on *thin ice* in my recovery?
- In what ways am I lying to myself about my current commitment to the long road of recovery?
- What growth am I resisting in my recovery?
- What are the next bold steps in my recovery?
- Am I committed to taking the necessary action steps to change, as I become aware of my progress or lack thereof?

Assignment: Read through all six suggestions for re-igniting your passion and take time this week to do these tasks. Consider how you can implement some of these tools into your daily lifestyle, increasing your commitment to your recovery.

Week 28:
Life After Lust Reading:

Three Tales of Temptation

Skill to Master #34: Practicing the recovery principle of "one day at a time"

Assignment: Write down three recovery lessons you learned from *each* tale in this week's reading. Commit to working your recovery "one day at a time," for the rest of your life.

Week 29:

<u>Skill to Master #32:</u> Connecting with the legitimate needs driving my addictive cravings

<u>Skill to Master #33:</u> Learning to ask for what I need

<u>Assignment:</u> Take notes throughout this week, writing down each time you experience a craving or desire to lust or act out. Try to connect with yourself in those moments, writing down your guess about which legitimate need may be driving your desires. Examples could be: sleep, connection (with people or spiritually), reassurance, rest, play, a good cry, etc. Then, rather than giving in to the craving or thought, look for how you can meet your legitimate need in a healthy way (which may include asking for what you need from others), as soon as you are able. Write down what you did each time.

Week 30:
<u>Life After Lust Reading:</u>

A Connected Christmas: Avoiding Auto-Pilot and Making Today Meaningful

<u>Skill to Master #30:</u> Connecting with my reasons for fighting for my recovery

<u>Assignment:</u> Write and then leave yourself a voicemail based on the structure provided in this week's reading. Ask others who care about you (such as your partner and accountability group) to leave you voicemails that you can keep for moments of weakness. Use the voicemail at least once this week in a moment of need. You can keep these voicemails indefinitely.

Week 31:
Life After Lust Reading:

What's Your Recovery Anthem?

Skill to Master #23: Connecting with my values

Assignment: Find your recovery anthem this week. Even better, start building a recovery playlist or CD and listen to it often.

Week 32:
Life After Lust Reading:

Introduction to Mastery section

Mission to Accomplish #2: Sustaining recovery with the promise of a meaningful future in mind

Assignment: Print out the complete list of *Skills to Master* found at LifeAfterLust.com and place them somewhere you will see them on a daily basis. Based on your understanding of recovery thus far, what *Skills to Master* would you add to this list? Commit to memorizing this list over the next month. Are you committed to the long yet rewarding road to *mastery* in recovery?

Recommended Resources:

Mastery: The Keys to Success and Long-term Fulfillment (Leonard, 1992)

The Power of Habit: Why We Do What We Do in Life and Business (Duhigg, 2012)

Week 33:

Essential Mindset #10: I will not exchange one addiction for another.

Assignment: Robert Weiss, LCSW, CSAT-S, shares this wisdom:

> *Battling cross- and co-occurring disorders can feel a bit like playing a game of addiction-related whack-a-mole. One addiction pops up, and while you're busy pounding it down another problem emerges. The game is even tougher when co-occurring behaviors are heavily intertwined... In such cases, relapse with one addiction nearly always leads to a quick relapse in the other.*[251]

Examine your current lifestyle choices. As you gain sexual sobriety, are other addictions taking the place of your sexual addiction? Alcohol, gambling, food, smoking, sugar, entertainment, drugs, gaming, workaholism, social media, etc? I call all of these behaviors *disconnecting behaviors* because they are simply other ways to numb out, distract, and temporarily escape. That is the old way of life. Recovery from all addictions will need to happen if long-term healing from sexual addiction is to occur. Learning the connection and self-care skills in this book along with getting professional help (as needed) will make this endeavor much more possible, addressing the roots of all addictions that are present.

Recommended Resource:

Healing Through Connection Workbook (Benedict - Coming soon for public use)

No Stones: Women Redeemed from Sexual Addiction (Ferree, 2010)

Facing the Shadow [3rd Edition] (Carnes, 2015)

Week 34:
Life After Lust Reading:

Connected Sex: A Paradigm Shift for the Sexually Addicted

Essential Mindset #12: I will learn to have a healthy relationship with my sexuality, rather than using it addictively.

Skill to Master #22: Practicing a healthy, connected sexuality

Assignment: As this week's chapter states, "successful recovery necessitates a new view of sexuality." The old one objectifies, the new one connects. Therapy with a sexual addiction therapist is recommended as you learn how to have a connected sexuality because they can guide you through the process of deepening all forms of connection (e.g. emotional, sexual) without using your partner as an object of lust or simply for personal gratification or release. A therapist can also help single sex addicts learn how to have a healthy sexuality. Sexual abuse survivors would especially benefit from getting additional professional help.

Are you committed to learning how to have a healthy relationship with sexuality, experiencing it as source of connection rather than addiction? Are you willing to get help in this area? Pick one of these resources to begin learning more about healthy, connected sexuality:

The Couple's Guide to Intimacy: How Sexual Reintegration Therapy Can Help Your Relationship Heal (Bercaw & Bercaw, 2010)

Love Sense: The Revolutionary New Science of Romantic Relationships (Johnson, 2013)

Sex Addiction as Affect Dysregulation (Katehakis, 2016) - See the table *Addictive Sex vs Healthy Sex* and pages 286-303.

Healing the Wounds of Sexual Addiction (Laaser, 2004) Pages 181-182

Week 35:

<u>Skill to Master #21:</u> Learning to emotionally connect with my partner.

<u>Assignment:</u> Learning to connect with your partner will be difficult and will require help, work, and patience. A good starting point is understanding how and why you disconnect in relationships. Whether you are in a relationship or single, take some time to take the online *Love Style Quiz* (https://www.howwelove.com/love-style-quiz/) to help you begin to understand your challenges with connecting to others. While you are on that site, download the *Comfort Circle Guide for the Listener* (in "Freebies"). This is one of many tools for connecting with your partner emotionally. Finding a daily connection exercise to practice with your partner will be important.

As mentioned previously, many couples will benefit from doing attachment based couple's therapy with a trained sexual addiction therapist. This allows the opportunity to work through relationship challenges, rebuild trust after betrayal, and learn/practice connection skills. The hope of a couple recovering together is that they can co-create a relationship much deeper than what most couple's experience.[252] As Katehakis writes, "The painful and difficult business of recovery from SA (sex addiction) often generates an entirely new intimacy and a joy never known by either party."[253]

This week, find a book that helps you learn more about fostering an intimate, emotional connection with your partner (or others, if single). I highly recommend *How We Love* by Milan & Kay Yerkovich (2006).

Recommended Resource:

Free to Attach

http://attachmentcounselor.com/community-resources/

Week 36:

Skill to Master #24: Prioritizing important relationships

Mission to Accomplish #10: Maintaining a connected relationship with my children

Assignment: For the recovering sex addict, learning to connect with one's children (or anyone for that matter) is a challenge.

This is going to be a learning experience, especially if your parents did not form a secure attachment with you. In her chapter on *Giving Your Child What You Never Got*, Dr Jonice Webb points out how "you haven't been able to offer your own children the emotional strengths that you didn't have yourself." For those of us who experienced childhood emotional neglect, Webb offers suggestions regarding parental guilt and provides strategies for being a connected parent. Another resource for parents that is attachment focused is called *How We Love Our Kids* by Milan & Kay Yerkovich (2011).

This week, find a book that helps you learn more about fostering a secure, emotional connection with your children (or future children). I recommend the two books mentioned this week (the first one was *Running On Empty*). If you are not a parent, write about how your connection with your parents (or lack thereof) impacted your ability to connect with others. If you are a parent, schedule routine time to connect with *each* of your kids, preferably on a daily basis. If your children are grown, it is not too late. There is still time to learn how to connect with your children.

Week 37:
Life After Lust Reading:

The Time Travelers: Making Changes that Matter

Skill to Master #20: Changing my present behavior as I connect with my future self

Assignment: Write down your answers to the questions in this week's chapter. Do the letter writing exercise and the visualization exercise (preferably under the direction of a therapist, especially if you are emotionally fragile). Write about what these experiences were like for you and how they impacted your view of the future. What changes do you want to make in the present as a result of doing these exercises?

Week 38:
Life After Lust Reading:

Holiday Recipes for Relapse and Recovery

Skill to Master #26: Maintaining recovery structure and self-care over the holidays

Assignment: After reading about the *Recipes for Relapse*, write down your biggest triggers over the holidays. Create a plan now for the next major holiday based on the *Recipes of Recovery* presented in this week's reading. Put your plan somewhere you will remember it for when the holiday arrives. After following through with your plan, modify it for the next approaching holiday. Plan to repeat this proactive practice whenever needed throughout each year. Eventually you may choose to have a set plan for each major holiday.

Week 39:
Life After Lust Reading:

Four Strategies for a Successful Summer Vacation

Skill to Master #27: Maintaining recovery structure and self-care on vacation

Assignment: After reading this week's chapter, think about how your addiction has manifested on past vacations and out of town travel. What temptations are the most predictable for you? Which of the strategies presented in this chapter are you the *most* likely and the *least* likely to do on your next vacation? How can you increase your partner's confidence that you will remain on track with your recovery on your next vacation?

Week 40:
Life After Lust Reading:

The Ripple Effects of Living in Alignment

Mission to Accomplish #9: Learning to live in alignment with my values

Assignment: Write out the answers to all of the questions posed in this week's chapter. How does the concept of *living in alignment* contrast with living the secretive life that accompanied your addiction? What could be the future benefits of learning to live a more aligned life now? What are the top five values you want to guide your life (humility, courage, honesty, love, authenticity, etc). Write these down and review them often.

Week 41:
Life After Lust Reading:

12 Porn Free Years: The Secrets of My Success

Skill to Master #1: Achieving long-term sobriety

Assignment: Write out the answers to all of the questions posed in this week's reading. What percentage of these lessons and recovery skills are you working on in your own recovery? What is it like to read the lessons and stories I've shared throughout this book? Find a story of another recovering sex addict and read it to increase feelings of hope and inspiration.

Recommended Reading:

Naked in Public: A Memoir of Recovery from Sex Addiction and Other Temporary Insanities (Sprout, 2015) - for females

Ashamed No More: A Pastor's Journey Through Sex Addiction (Ryan, 2012) - for males

Week 42:
Life After Lust Reading:

Out of Our Pain Comes Our Purpose

Mission to Accomplish #1: Finding my purpose as I recover from my pain

Assignment: Answer these questions presented in this week's reading - Are you willing to do the deep and difficult work of recovery today, holding tightly to the belief that you will benefit tomorrow? Are you willing to postpone present pleasure and persevere through present pain for the hope of future satisfaction? Take a few minutes to imagine what future purpose could grow out of your present and past pain. Draw a picture or make a collage of this hopeful future reality and put it somewhere you will see it often.

Week 43:

Life After Lust Reading:

Introduction to Mission section

Essential Mindset #5: As I recover from my sexual addiction, I will connect with a greater mission.

Assignment: Print out the complete list of *Missions to Accomplish* found at LifeAfterLust.com and place them somewhere you will see them on a daily basis. Based on your understanding of recovery, what *Missions to Accomplish* would you add to this list? Commit to memorizing this list over the next month.

Assignment: Explain how addiction has impacted each of these areas:

- Your belief in yourself
- Your personal goals
- Your hope for the future
- You desire to help others
- How might recovery impact all four of those areas?
- If healing from addiction increases your courage, aligns you with your values, and increases your belief in living a bigger life, what dreams would you want to accomplish?

Week 44:

Life After Lust Reading:

Dear Porn: A Father's Letter

Mission to Accomplish #12: Proactively protecting the younger generation from the threats of pornography

Assignment: Take a few minutes to watch the video version of *Dear Porn: A Father's Letter* (Available at LifeAfterLust.com). As you read this week's chapter and watched the video, what emotions did you experience? Do you sense the urgency for protecting the younger generation from pornography's influence? Which protection tactics that were presented in this piece are you committed to pursuing? Check out the Fight the New Drug (fightthenewdrug.org) website to explore possible ways you can support the younger generation in their battle against pornography. If the *Dear Porn* video strengthened your recovery resolve and desire to protect the younger generation, I invite you to add watching it to your daily recovery rituals.

Week 45:

Life After Lust Reading:

Vote for Love

Mission to Accomplish #3: Standing against businesses that profit from the porn industry

Mission to Accomplish #4: Opposing the porn industry in my streets, my home, and my heart

Assignment: Think about the following excerpt from this week's reading:

> *Gassing up at a station that peddles porn may not register as wrong. But I have resisted this for years, regardless of price. I have also often avoided buying from a local big-name bookstore because their explicit books are visible to adolescent eyes. I've long bypassed convenient coffee and the best looking burgers when sold to the public through seduction. I know I vote with every transaction; supporting a porn selling business means supporting the porn industry. I refuse to give them my stamp of approval.*

Now, think about all of the places you do business - the stores, restaurants, gas stations, movie theaters, websites, etc. Which ones sell pornography or promote sexual exploitation in any form? Would you consider stopping your indirect or direct support of the porn industry by stopping doing business wherever the porn industry benefits in any way? Would you go a step further and let those businesses know why you are not doing business with them? How else could you *vote for love* instead of lust in your streets, home, and heart? Remember, your vote matters!

Week 46:
Life After Lust Reading:

What One Person Can Do to Stand Against "Shades of Grey"

Mission to Accomplish #6: Finding the courage to stand for my deepest convictions

Mission to Accomplish #7: Standing against objectification and sexual exploitation

Mission to Accomplish #8: Actively working to raise my community's standards regarding all forms of pornography

Assignment: This article presented six ways you can stand against movies like *Fifty Shades of Grey* that promote pornographic content and abusive attitudes. Write about how you can practically engage in each of these strategies both in your community and globally:

1. Let your money talk
2. Put it in writing (See "Letter to Theater" in Appendix B)
3. Invest in good
4. Spread the word
5. Join the movement
6. Persist and believe

I invite you to support change by joining the *Anti-Pornography Movement*, partnering with organizations like The National Center on Sexual Exploitation, Fight the New Drug, and coalitions against pornography. I have also created *The Anti-Pornography Movement* Facebook group for those seeking to connect and share resources. Collectively, we can make a difference!

Recommended Resources:

National Center on Sexual Exploitation
http://endsexualexploitation.org/ (See Dirty Dozen List)

Fight the New Drug - http://fightthenewdrug.org

The LoneSTAR Coalition Against Pornography(LCAP)
https://lonestarcoalitionagainstporn.org/about/

Utah Coalition Against Pornography (UCAP)
https://utahcoalition.org

Porn Harms Facebook Page
https://www.facebook.com/PornHarms/

The Anti-Porn Movement Facebook Group
https://www.facebook.com/groups/TheAntiPornMovement/

Week 47:
Life After Lust Reading:

Defending Against Prelapse: From Passivity to Passion

Essential Mindset #17 (repeated): I will maintain my recovery momentum by actively opposing passivity and fueling my passion.

Assignment: After reading this week's chapter again, revisit your recovery focused mission statement. Could it use any revisions based on what you've learned from your recovery journey? After revising your mission statement, type it up, print it, frame it, and hang it somewhere you will see it often. Share your recovery mission statement with your partner and with your group, giving them permission to let you know when your recovery commitments begin to wane.

Week 48:

Life After Lust Reading:

The Wake-Up Call

Mission to Accomplish #13: *Waking up and taking action when my recovery commitments begin to wane*

Assignment: How did you emotionally respond to the story about my wake-up call in the waves? Looking over the pitfalls of long-term recovery, which ones do you relate to the most? What pitfalls of long-term recovery would you add to this list? Looking over the possibilities of long-term recovery, which ones inspire you the most? Based on your current recovery commitment, how many of the pitfalls and possibilities do you think will result from your current behavior? Have you woken up in your recovery? If not, what will it take to wake you up? Will you choose to wake up now?

Week 49:

Skill to Master #28: Making worthy memories

Mission to Accomplish #15: Creating a legacy for future generations

Assignment: In *The Wake-Up Call* you read that "learning to let go of lust, we can connect with the mission to move beyond our destiny, creating a legacy of love for generations to come." Write two to three pages on the person you want to become through recovery, the memories you want to make while you're on this earth, and the legacy you want to leave for your children and future generations. Share this with your partner and with your group.

Week 50:

Mission to Accomplish #14: Maintaining long-term recovery

Assignment: As you consider your progress through this *Recovery Roadmap*, compile a list of the tools that were most meaningful and helpful to you. Looking ahead, which ones will help you maintain long-term recovery? How can you build these healthy habits into your daily routines, if you have not done so already?

Week 51:
Life After Lust Reading:

Conclusion

Assignment: After reading this week's chapter, do you feel more motivated or inspired? What other feelings did you experience when you finished the book? Have you embraced the challenge to rise up and live out life after lust?

Week 52:

Congratulations are in order. This is the last week of your first year pursuing life after lust! What healthy activity can you do to celebrate? Plan it and execute it. Then, I challenge you to begin the 52-week plan again. This will deepen your understanding and widen your experiences that will lead you to lasting change.

Starting over is also symbolic, since the reality is *there is no finish line in recovery*. It is a life-long process.

Assignment: If you were inspired by the contents of this book, consider passing along the inspiration to others by buying a copy for someone else who would benefit. Ask yourself what other ways you can give back to others as a result of your growth. Is there someone you could mentor or sponsor, passing on to them the lessons you've learned in recovery?

I would love to hear how this book has impacted you. I can be reached at forest@forestbenedict.com. Also, I invite you to join the *Life After Lust Community* Facebook group at www.facebook.com/groups/LifeAfterLust.

I honor you for the work you have chosen to do as you pursue recovery. The world is a better place because of it. Stay the course. You are worth it.

Appendix A

What I Am Worth

An adaptation of "What My Wife Is Worth," modified by Avalon Vic on

https://crushingthelion.com/2016/06/27/what-i-am-worth/

I am a woman of infinite worth. Because of this, I deserve my husband's best efforts.

I deserve a husband who only has eyes for me.

I deserve a husband in active recovery, not passively going with the flow.

I deserve a husband who reminds me that I am not to blame for his past or present choices.

I deserve a husband who actively opposes visual and mental lust in all forms; viewing it as the enemy of true intimacy.

I deserve a husband who is trustworthy, both when I am looking and when I'm unaware.

I deserve a husband who seeks help when needed, remaining accountable to those who call out his greatness and strength.

I deserve a husband with the courage to face his deepest fears, inadequacies, and wounds for the sake of his healing.

I deserve a husband who learns from his mistakes, creating and communicating new plans for change.

I deserve a husband who is learning how to connect and does the hard work in spite of insecurities and inadequacies in this area.

I deserve a husband who tells the truth about his behavior and is honest when his heart wants to wander.

I deserve a husband who does whatever it takes to change whatever wounds me.

I deserve a husband who takes responsibility for his life, rather than being a victim of circumstances, feelings, or personal history.

I deserve a husband who progresses in personal growth; who is becoming the man he's told me he wants to be.

I deserve a husband who is committed to perseverance and course correction; who gets up quickly after failures.

I deserve a husband who cares for himself so that he can offer me more presence and participation in daily life.

I deserve a husband who models faith, purity, passion, and purpose to our children.

I deserve a husband who acknowledges his imperfections yet resists using them as justifications for a small life.

I deserve a husband who fights for my heart.

I deserve a husband who pursues my emotional and physical safety.

I deserve a husband who cherishes me, pursues me, and defends me.

I deserve a husband who humbly responds to my personal boundaries and listens to the pain his choices have caused.

I deserve a husband who remains patient when forgiveness and trust do not come quickly.

I deserve a husband who desires me, cutting off opportunities to seek all counterfeit connections.

I deserve a husband who nurtures me, encourages me to use my gifts, and empowers me to come alive.

I deserve a husband who supports my needs for relationships, relaxation, rest, and rejuvenation.

I deserve a husband who serves me, looking for ways to lighten my load.

I deserve a husband who is eager to invest both his time and attention.

I deserve a husband who sees me, knows me, and loves me.

I deserve a husband who reminds me every day that my value does not depend on my weight, my style, my sexiness or sexual availability, how I was treated as a child, or any other outside factor.

I deserve a husband who reminds me that I am beautiful and I am enough.

My worth is innate and cannot be tarnished.

I deserve all of these things because I am a woman of infinite worth.

Appendix B

Sample Movie Theater Letter

Dear Manager of _____ Theater,

It has come to my attention that you are planning to show the upcoming movie *Fifty Shades of Grey* in your movie theater. As a concerned parent and citizen in our community, I believe that the messages in this movie glamorize sexual violence and dehumanize men and women.

A study published in the Journal of Women's Health in 2013 examined themes in *Fifty Shades of Grey*, with the help of abuse and sexual practice experts. The results revealed that the book has extensive instances of emotional abuse, sexual violence, and reactions by the victim that are typical of abused women. The conclusion of the study was this:

"Our analysis identified patterns in *Fifty Shades* that reflect pervasive intimate partner violence—one of the biggest problems of our time. Further, our analysis adds to a growing body of literature noting dangerous violence standards being perpetuated in popular culture."

I cannot in good conscience support any establishment that spreads messages such as this through the showing of *Fifty Shades of Grey* or movies like it. Pervasive pornography already has a stranglehold on our society and I believe this movie perpetuates messages that hurt all of us, especially the most vulnerable, our children.

For these reasons I am choosing to protest the decision to show this movie by refraining from attending your theater **for as long as** *Fifty Shades* **is shown there**. Instead, I will choose to support theaters that are not showing the movie. Additionally, I will donate my movie ticket money toward local domestic violence shelters and toward causes that perpetuate love, human worth, and healthy sexuality. This issue is so important to me that I am encouraging my family, friends, and others in my sphere of influence to do the same.

Please know that I do not have anything against you personally. I have enjoyed my movie-going experience at your theater in the past. I am only doing what I believe to be right; standing up for the good of our community and our world.

Should you make any changes in response to this letter or others like it, please let me know so that I can thank you publicly and commence attending your theater. Thank you for any consideration you give to this important issue.

Sincerely,

Your Name and Title (if relevant)

Email Address

Acknowledgements

Much like my recovery, writing this book was harder than I thought it would be. Also like recovery, this book required a community effort. I am grateful for the contributions, support, guidance, and encouragement of many people.

To my wife Stacie — Thank you for your encouragement, support, investments of time and resources, and love you've shown me throughout this book writing process. Thank you for joining me on this recovery journey. You truly are worth a lifetime of my best connection and recovery efforts.

To my boys — I am so grateful that I get to be your daddy. I will strive to live out the principles presented in this book and do my best to prepare you to defend against addiction in your own lives. You too are worth my best connection and recovery efforts and I will do my part to change the world you are growing up in.

To those who helped clarify my words in this book — Marcy Pusey, Jody L. Collins, and Michelle Linford, I am so grateful. A big thanks to the folks at HSP for your amazing cover design and formatting services.

To those who encouraged my writing — Thank you Mike Roubicek and Stacey Thacker for supporting my big ideas and helping me thrive as a therapist and writer. I am grateful too for an endless list of encouragers and supporters including Gary Sells, Dorina Gilmore-Young, Denise Quirk, Jason Fuller, Gary Moline, Michael Regier, Staci Sprout, Daniel Bunker, Josh & Karen Huckaby, Melody Bergman, and many others.

To those who played key roles in the journey that led me here — Mom, thank you for supporting me and my writing throughout my whole life. Your love and generosity have shaped me in so many ways. Papa, thank you for doing your best and for believing in big dreams. Blossom, thank you for showing me what's possible, encouraging me, and being a model of the "big magic" that can come through creativity and vision. Todd Frye, thank you for training me to do this work and letting me lead the SATP program. Thank you Clint Yarbrough, Invia Betjoseph, Mary Anne Fifield, Shane Adamson, Todd Bellinger, Ericlee Gilmore, Mark Barnes, Mary Shamshoian, Dr Rose, Delores Friesen, my friends and family, and all of the anonymous warriors who have held my arms up when they were too weak and who continue to do so.

To my clients - thank you for challenging me, teaching me, and trusting me.

To my Abba — I belong to you. Thank you for finding this lost boy, leading me into healing, and giving me what lust never will.

Endnotes

[1] The Twelve Steps – *Sexaholics anonymous*. (1982). Retrieved from http://www.sa.org/steps/

[2] It is recommended that anyone engaging in sexual behavior that feels out of control, compulsive, or results in the harm of self or others consult a certified sexual addiction therapist who can assess for the presence of a sexual addiction and provide treatment. In *Your Recovery Roadmap: A 52 Week Plan* you will find information about finding a sexual addiction therapist and/or sexual addiction treatment program that fits your needs.

[3] Quotes by Jim Rohn, America's Foremost Business Philosopher, reprinted with permission from SUCCESS ©2016. As a world-renowned author and success expert, Jim Rohn touched millions of lives during his 46-year career as a motivational speaker and messenger of positive life change. For more information on Jim and his popular personal achievement resources or to subscribe to the weekly Jim Rohn Newsletter, visit www.JimRohn.com or www.SUCCESS.com

[4] McGonigal, K. (2012). *The Neuroscience of Change: A Compassion-Based Program for Personal Transformation*. Sounds True.

[5] Daw Holloway, J. (2005). *Guilt can do good*. American Psychological Association, 36(19), 22. Retrieved from http://www.apa.org/monitor/nov05/guilt.aspx

[6] Carnes, P. (2001). *Out of the shadows: understanding sexual addiction*. Center City, MN: Hazelden

[7] The Holy Bible: New International Version. (2011). Colorado Springs, CO: Biblica. Romans 12:2

[8] Benedict, F. (2015). *My path out of porn addiction: a therapist's journey*. Retrieved from https://lifestarcentralvalley.wordpress.com/2015/04/22/my-path-out-of-porn-addiction-a-therapists-journey/
Benedict, F. (2015). *My path out of porn addiction: a therapist's journey*. Retrieved from http://www.fresnobee.com/opinion/readers-opinion/article20947515.html

[9] Frye, T., *Neurology of sexual addiction*. (2010). Retrieved from https://www.youtube.com/watch?v=LVRcz-69los&t=73s

[10] Carnes, P. (2013, July). Lecture presented at LifeSTYLE Intervention Conference, Las Vegas, Nevada

[11] Daum, K. (2016). *17 Arnold palmer quotes that inspire success.* Retrieved from http://www.inc.com/kevin-daum/17-arnold-palmer-quotes-that-inspire-success.html

[12] Benedict, F. (2016, June 29). *Don't be a victim to your porn addiction.* Retrieved from https://www.xxxchurch.com/men/dont-victim-porn-addiction.html

[13] Laaser, M. R. (2011). *The 7 principles of highly accountable men.* Kansas City, MO: Beacon Hill Press of Kansas City.

[14] Marcinko, R. (1992). *Rogue warrior.* New York, NY u.a.: Pocket Books.

[15] 1 Corinthians 10:13; Holy Bible, NIV

[16] Matthew 7:7; Holy Bible, NIV

[17] Deut. 30:19; Holy Bible, NIV

[18] Lust. [Def. 2]. (n.d.) *Merriam-Webster Online.* In Merriam-Webster.http://www.merriam-webster.com/dictionary/lust

[19] Proverbs 27:20; Holy Bible, NIV

[20] McGonigal, K. (2012). *The willpower instinct: how self-control works, why it matters, and what you can do to get more of it.* New York: Avery.

[21] Sexaholics Anonymous. (2001). *Why stop lusting?* Retrieved from https://www.sa.org/content.php?name=whystop

[22] Sexaholics Anonymous. (2001). *Why stop lusting?* Retrieved from https://www.sa.org/content.php?name=whystop

[23] Sill, E. R. (2009). *"A man takes a drink...then the drink takes the man".* Retrieved from http://www.barrypopik.com/index.php/new_york_city/entry/a_man_takes_a_drinkthen_the_drink_takes_the_man

[24] *St. Augustine Confessions* - Book Eight. (n.d.).

[25] Shakespeare, W. *Venus and Adonis* p. 799-804

[26] Sexaholics Anonymous. (1989-2002). *Sexaholics anonymous.* SA Literature.

[27] Hilton, D. L. (2009). *He restoreth my soul: understanding and breaking the chemical and spiritual chains of pornography addiction through the atonement of jesus christ.* San Antonio, TX: Forward Press Pub.

[28] Sprout, S., (2017, January 15). [E-mail].

[29] Conference created by Jennifer Lamprey, CEO of *I Love My Body Diet, Inc.*

[30] Carnes, P. (2001). *Out of the shadows: understanding sexual addiction.* Center City, MN: Hazelden

[31] Gray, D, Olson, T., LifeSTAR Program (Phase 1)

[32] Right Turn. (2013, September 11). *Euphoric recall in addiction: a "built in forgetter".* Retrieved from http://www.right-turn.org/euphoric-recall-in-addiction-a-built-in-forgetter/

[33] Hook, J. N., Hook, J. P., & Hines, S. (2008). *Reach out or act out: long-term group therapy for sexual addiction.* Sexual Addiction & Compulsivity, 15(3), 217-232.

[34] McGonigal, K. (2012, February 01). *The willpower instinct.* Retrieved from https://www.youtube.com/watch?v=V5BXuZL1HAg&t=1s

[35] *Adult children: alcoholic/dysfunctional families.* (2006). Torrance, CA: Adult Children of Alcoholics World Service Organization.

[36] Benedict, F. (2015, April 01). *Defending against "pre-lapse": moving from complacency to commitment.* Retrieved from https://lifestarcentralvalley.wordpress.com/2015/04/01/defending-against-pre-lapse-moving-from-complacency-to-commitment/

Benedict, F. (2015, December 30). *From passivity to passion: the next level of your recovery in the new year*. Retrieved from https://lifestarcentralvalley.wordpress.com/2015/12/30/from-passivity-to-passion-the-next-level-of-your-recovery-in-the-new-year/

[37] Carnes, P. (2015, September 30). *Dr patrick carnes, leading sex addiction expert, video interview*. Retrieved from https://www.youtube.com/watch?v=m7TwURjJo80

[38] Marcinko, R. (1992). *Rogue warrior*. New York, NY u.a.: Pocket Books.

[39] Yeats, W.B.. (n.d.).

[40] Benedict, F. (2013, March 24). *From under the rock*. Retrieved from https://lifestarcentralvalley.wordpress.com/2013/03/24/from-under-the-rock-by-forest-benedict-m-a-satp-c-lifestar-of-the-central-valley/.

*Some suggestions inspired by LifeSTAR Co-Founder Dan Gray's "Humble Warrior Heart" lecture.

[41] Sexaholics Anonymous. (1989-2002). *Sexaholics anonymous*. SA Literature. 69.

[42] *Alcoholics anonymous*. (1939). New York: Works Pub. Co. 58-60.

[43] TLC (2005) - *Aron ralston describes the amputation*. Retrieved from https://www.youtube.com/watch?v=B2XLoQ1xYB0

[44] Ralston, A. (2004). *Between a rock and a hard place*. New York: Atria Books. 285.

[45] Sexaholics Anonymous. (1989-2002). *Sexaholics anonymous*. SA Literature. 104.

[46] Sexaholics Anonymous. (1989-2002). *Sexaholics anonymous*. SA Literature. 104

[47] Leonard, G. (1992). *Mastery: the keys to success and long-term fulfillment*. New York: Plume.

[48] Boyd, L. (2015, December 15). *After watching this, your brain will not be the same*. Retrieved from https://www.youtube.com/watch?v=LNHBMFCzznE&spfreload=5

[49] Boyd, L. (2015, December 15). *After watching this, your brain will not be the same*. Retrieved from https://www.youtube.com/watch?v=LNHBMFCzznE&spfreload=5

[50] Webb, J. (2012). *Running on empty: overcome your childhood emotional neglect*. New York: Morgan James Publishing.

[51] Steurer, G. (2013, October 24). *LifeStar is REAL recovery for pornography and sexual addiction*. Retrieved from https://www.youtube.com/watch?v=Ydhpz7CFnRE&t=2s

[52] Steurer, G., source unknown

[53] Benedict, F. *(2015, August 26) Dear mr. duggar: when sexual secrets surface*. Retrieved from https://lifestarcentralvalley.wordpress.com/2015/08/26/dear-mr-duggar-when-sexual-secrets-surface/

Benedict, F. (2015, September 4). *Forest benedict: when sex secrets surface*. Retrieved from http://www.fresnobee.com/opinion/readers-opinion/article33828192.html

[54] Moraski, L. (2015, August 20). *Josh duggar releases statement following ashley madison scandal*. Retrieved from http://www.cbsnews.com/news/josh-duggar-releases-statement-following-ashley-madison-scandal/

[55] McGonigal, K. (2012, February 01). *The willpower instinct*. Retrieved from https://www.youtube.com/watch?v=V5BXuZL1HAg&t=1s

[56] Hifler, J. S. (1992). *A Cherokee feast of days: daily meditations* (Vol. 1). Tulsa, OK: Council Oak Books.

[57] Skinner, K., Steurer, G. (2012). *Strengthening recovery through strengthening marriage: healing from pornography addiction*.

58 McGonigal, K. (2012). *The neuroscience of change: a compassion-based program for personal transformation.* Sounds True.

59 Donehey, M., Ingram, J., & Owen, J. (2010). *Healing begins* [MP3]. Conservatory Park: Reunion Records.

60 Laaser, M. (2015). Lecture presented in the SATP program, Mid-America Nazarene University (online)

61 Internet Pornography Statistics. (2006-2008). Retrieved from http://www.mykidsbrowser.com/pornography_stats.php

62 Internet Pornography Statistics - TopTenREVIEWS. (2014). Retrieved from http://www.toptenreviews.com/internet-pornography-statistics/

63 Reid, R. C., & Woolley, S. R. (2006). Using emotionally focused therapy for couples to resolve attachment ruptures created by hypersexual behavior. *Sexual Addiction & Compulsivity, 13*(2-3), 219-239.

64 Reid, R. C., & Woolley, S. R. (2006). Using emotionally focused therapy for couples to resolve attachment ruptures created by hypersexual behavior. *Sexual Addiction & Compulsivity, 13*(2-3), 219-239.

65 Revelation 2:4; Holy Bible, NIV

66 Zillmann, D., & Bryant, J. (1988). Pornography's impact on sexual satisfaction1. *Journal of Applied Social Psychology, 18*(5), 438-453.

67 Castleman, M. (2010, May 28). *Premature ejaculation: the two causes of men's #1 sex problem.* Retrieved from https://www.psychologytoday.com/blog/all-about-sex/201005/premature-ejaculation-the-two-causes-mens-1-sex-problem

68 Deem, G. (2014, June 9). *Porn: many teens watch it, and two reasons that's a problem.* Retrieved from http://www.huffingtonpost.com/gabe-deem/porn-many-teens-watch-it-_b_5450478.html

69 Doidge, N. (2007). *The brain that changes itself: stories of personal triumph from the frontiers of brain science.* New York: Viking.

70 Bridges, A. J., Wosnitzer, R., Scharrer, E., Sun, C., & Liberman, R. (2010). Aggression and sexual behavior in best-selling pornography videos: A Content Analysis Update. *Violence Against Women, 16*(10), 1065-1085.

71 Weeks, N. (2010). *Effects of pornography on relationships.* Families & Communities. Retrieved from http://extension.usu.edu/files/publications/publication/FC_Marriage_2010-01pr.pdf

72 Sisterhood of Support. (2014, July 21). *Barbara steffens part 1.* Retrieved from https://www.youtube.com/watch?v=d3VkPLFgLZU

73 American Academy of Matrimonial Lawyers. (2002, November 14). *Is the internet bad for your marriage? online affairs, pornographic sites playing greater role in divorces.* Retrieved from http://www.prnewswire.com/news-releases/is-the-internet-bad-for-your-marriage-online-affairs-pornographic-sites-playing-greater-role-in-divorces-76826727.html

74 Hilton, D. L. (2009). *He restoreth my soul: understanding and breaking the chemical and spiritual chains of pornography addiction through the atonement of jesus christ.* San Antonio, TX: Forward Press Pub. 71.

75 Pornography and Sex Trafficking. (n.d.). *Trafficking within the professional porn industry.* Retrieved from http://stoptraffickingdemand.com/trafficking-within-the-industry/

76 Proverbs 5:8; Holy Bible, NIV

77 Manning, B. (2000). *Ruthless trust: the ragamuffin's path to god.* San Francisco: Harper.

[78] McGonigal, K. (2012, February 01). *The willpower instinct.* Retrieved from https://www.youtube.com/watch?v=V5BXuZL1HAg&t=1s

[79] Based on "secrecy is the lifeblood of addiction" by Dan Gray, LCSW, CSAT, Co-founder of the LifeStar Network. Retrieved from http://www.lifestarstgeorge.com/blog/?p=9

[80] Katehakis, A. (2013, June 19). *Telling your partner: the disclosure process in recovery from sex addiction.* Retrieved from https://psychcentral.com/blog/archives/2013/06/19/telling-your-partner-the-disclosure-process-in-recovery-from-sex-addiction/

[81] Steurer, G. (2016). SATP interview [Personal interview]. Based on the research of both Geoff Steurer, LMFT and Jeff Ford, LMFT

[82] Steurer, G. (2010, March 30). *The importance of disclosure.* Retrieved from http://www.lifestarstgeorge.com/blog/?p=31

[83] John 8:32; Holy Bible, NIV

[84] Benedict, F. (2016, March 18). *The paradox of pornography addiction: what you fear most will heal you.* Retrieved from https://www.xxxchurch.com/men/paradox-pornography-addiction-fear-will-heal.html

[85] Frye, T. (2010, September 27). *Intimacy disorder and sexual addiction.* Retrieved from https://www.youtube.com/watch?v=KeXfs2A84Hs&t=137s

[86] Frye, T. (2010, September 27). *Intimacy disorder and sexual addiction.* Retrieved from https://www.youtube.com/watch?v=KeXfs2A84Hs&t=137s

[87] Sexaholics Anonymous. (1989-2002). Sexaholics Anonymous. SA Literature.

[88] Jung, C. "We are wounded in relationship and we heal through relationship" (source unknown). Said by Harville Herndrix as well.

[89] Benedict, F. (2014). *Healing Through Connection: A Blueprint for Long-Term Recovery* [Workbook]. LifeSTAR of the Central Valley, Fresno, CA.

[90] Benedict, F. (2016, May 25). *Five reasons to fire your accountability partner.* Retrieved from https://www.xxxchurch.com/men/5-reasons-fire-accountability-partner.html

[91] McGonigal, K. (2012). *The neuroscience of change: a compassion-based program for personal transformation.* Sounds True.

[92] Frye, T. (2010, September 27). *Intimacy disorder and sexual addiction.* Retrieved from https://www.youtube.com/watch?v=KeXfs2A84Hs&t=137s

[93] Ephesians 4:15; Holy Bible, NIV

[94] Benedict, F. (2015, July 26). *The neuroscience of self-care.* Retrieved from https://lifestarcentralvalley.wordpress.com/2015/07/26/the-neuroscience-of-self-care-stephen-kuhn-interviews-forest-benedict-satp-c-2/

Benedict, F. (2014, September 26). *The neuroscience of sleep: strengthening the brain to resist relapse.* https://lifestarcentralvalley.wordpress.com/2014/09/26/the-neuroscience-of-sleep-empowering-the-brain-to-resist-relapse/

Benedict, F. (2014, August 6). *Exercise: good for the body, great for the brain.* Retrieved from https://lifestarcentralvalley.wordpress.com/2014/08/06/exercise-good-for-the-body-great-for-the-brain/

Benedict, F. (2014, October 31). The scary side of sugar: the trick of treats. Retrieved from https://lifestarcentralvalley.wordpress.com/2014/10/31/the-scary-side-of-sugar/

*Themes from this article based on McGonigal, K. (2012, February 01). The Willpower Instinct. Retrieved from https://www.youtube.com/watch?v=V5BXuZL1HAg&t=1s

95 Benedict, F. (2015, July 11). My One Thing: Forest Benedict. Retrieved from http://www.beltoftruth.com/my-one-thing-forest-benedict/

96 Hilton, D. L. (2009). He restoreth my soul: understanding and breaking the chemical and spiritual chains of pornography addiction through the atonement of Jesus Christ. San Antonio, TX: Forward Press Pub. 71.

97 Hilton, D. J. (2010, September 08). Donald L. Hilton Jr., MD speaks to Youth and Parents about Pornography and its impact on the Brain. Retrieved from https://www.youtube.com/watch?v=0ADYe5w75yk

98 Carson, R. E. (2012). The brain fix: what's the matter with your gray matter. Deerfield Beach, FL: Health Communications. 214.

99 Carson, R. E. (2012). The brain fix: what's the matter with your gray matter. Deerfield Beach, FL: Health Communications. 214.

100 Carson, R. E. (2012). The brain fix: what's the matter with your gray matter. Deerfield Beach, FL: Health Communications.

101 McGonigal, K. (2012). The willpower instinct: how self-control works, why it matters, and what you can do to get more of it. New York: Avery.

102 Carson, R. E. (2012). The brain fix: what's the matter with your gray matter. Deerfield Beach, FL: Health Communications.

103 McGonigal, K. (2013, February 01). Brain Science - A Miracle Cure for Willpower. Retrieved from https://www.youtube.com/watch?v=gpk1kt2N5KI

104 Blankenship, R., & Laaser, M. (2004). Sexual Addiction and ADHD: Is There A Connection? Sexual Addiction & Compulsivity, 11(1-2), 7-20. doi:10.1080/10720160490458184

105 Henslin, E. R., & Johnson, B. F. (2008). This is your brain on joy: a revolutionary program for balancing mood, restoring brain health, and nurturing spiritual growth. Nashville, TN: Thomas Nelson

106 Ratey, J. J., & Hagerman, E. (2008). Spark: the revolutionary new science of exercise and the brain. New York: Little, Brown.

107 Ratey, J. J., & Hagerman, E. (2008). Spark: the revolutionary new science of exercise and the brain. New York: Little, Brown. 189.

108 Ratey, J. J., & Hagerman, E. (2008). Spark: the revolutionary new science of exercise and the brain. New York: Little, Brown. 190.

109 Veselak, C. (n.d.). Relapse and blood sugar dysregulation. Retrieved from http://docplayer.net/32705118-Relapse-and-blood-sugar-dysregulation-by-christina-veselak-lmft.html

110 McGonigal, K. (2012, February 01). The willpower instinct. Retrieved from https://www.youtube.com/watch?v=V5BXuZL1HAg&t=1s

111 Weiss, R. (2013, September 25). "Thanks for Sharing" Nails It With Cross-Addictions. Retrieved from https://www.psychologytoday.com/blog/love-and-sex-in-the-digital-age/201309/thanks-sharing-nails-it-cross-addictions

112 Weiss, R. (2013, September 25). "Thanks for Sharing" Nails It With Cross-Addictions. Retrieved from https://www.psychologytoday.com/blog/love-and-sex-in-the-digital-age/201309/thanks-sharing-nails-it-cross-addictions

113 McGonigal, K. (2012). The willpower instinct: how self-control works, why it matters, and what you can do to get more of it. New York: Avery.

[114] Gailliot, M., & Baumeister, R. (2007, November 1). The Physiology of Willpower: Linking Blood Glucose to Self-Control . Retrieved from http://psr.sagepub.com/content/11/4/303.abstract

[115] Carson, R. (2013, July). Lecture presented at LifeSTYLE Intervention Conference.

[116] Thompson, C. (2013, August 22). Curt Thompson: Neuroplasticity and Self-Control. Retrieved from https://www.youtube.com/watch?v=FdHzZZndOj8

[117] McGonigal, K. (2012, September 12). Learn: Mindfulness of Breathing. Retrieved from https://kellymcgonigal.wordpress.com/2012/09/12/mindfulness-of-breathing/

[118] McGonigal, K. (2010, April 28). Meditate Your Way to More Willpower. Retrieved from https://www.psychologytoday.com/blog/the-science-willpower/201004/meditate-your-way-more-willpower

[119] Loehr, J. E., & Schwartz, T. (2003). *The power of full engagement: managing energy, not time, is the key to high performance and personal renewal.* New York: Free Press.

[120] Benedict, F. (2016, July 15). *Permission to rest.* Retrieved from https://lifestarcentralvalley.wordpress.com/2016/07/15/permission-to-rest

[121] Flores, P. J. (2004). *Addiction as an attachment disorder.* Lanham: Jason Aronson.

[122] Webb, J. (2012). *Running on empty: overcome your childhood emotional neglect.* New York: Morgan James Publishing.

[123] Carnes, P. (1998). The Making of a Sex Addict. Retrieved from https://www.iitap.com/wp-content/uploads/2015/11/ARTICLE_The-Making-of-a-Sex-Addict_PCarnes.pdf Adapted from "The Obsessive Shadow"

[124] Webb, J. (2012). *Running on empty: overcome your childhood emotional neglect.* New York: Morgan James Publishing.

[125] *Adult children: alcoholic/dysfunctional families.* (2006). Torrance, CA: Adult Children of Alcoholics World Service Organization.

[126] Loehr, J. E., & Schwartz, T. (2003). *The power of full engagement: managing energy, not time, is the key to high performance and personal renewal.* New York: Free Press.

[127] Benedict, F. (2014, November 6). Dealing with "Demons": Healing from a Shame-Based Identity. Retrieved from https://lifestarcentralvalley.wordpress.com/2014/11/06/dealing-with-demons-healing-from-a-shame-based-identity/

[128] Brown, B. (2012, March 23). Brené Brown: Listening to shame: TED Talk: Inspiring: Informative: Ideas. Retrieved from https://www.youtube.com/watch?v=L0ifUM1DYKg

[129] Jung, C. (2009). *The Red Book* (1st ed.). W. W. Norton & Company.

[130] Frye, T. (2010, September 27). *Intimacy disorder and sexual addiction.* Retrieved from https://www.youtube.com/watch?v=KeXfs2A84Hs&t=137s

[131] Carnes, P. (2001). *Out of the shadows: Understanding sexual addiction.* Center City, MN: Hazelden

[132] Lemieux, C. (2014, February 5). Brené Brown Talks to The Shriver Report: The Power of Shame on Women Living on the Brink. Retrieved from http://shriverreport.org/how-to-overcome-shame-when-on-the-brink-brene-brown/

[133] Bradshaw, J. (2012, October 7). The Role of Shame in Addiction. Retrieved from https://www.themeadows.com/blog/item/152-the-role-of-shame-in-addiction

[134] Steurer, G. (2013, October 24). *LifeStar is REAL recovery for pornography and sexual addiction.* Retrieved from https://www.youtube.com/watch?v=Ydhpz7CFnRE&t=2s

[135] Center for Building a Culture of Empathy. (n.d.). Culture of Empathy Builder: Brené Brown. Retrieved from http://cultureofempathy.com/references/Experts/Brene-Brown.htm

[136] McGonigal, K. (2012, February 01). *The willpower instinct*. Retrieved from https://www.youtube.com/watch?v=V5BXuZL1HAg&t=1s

[137] Engel, B. (2013, July 14). How Compassion Can Heal Shame from Childhood. Retrieved from https://www.psychologytoday.com/blog/the-compassion-chronicles/201307/how-compassion-can-heal-shame-childhood

[138] Engel, B. (2013, July 14). How Compassion Can Heal Shame from Childhood. Retrieved from https://www.psychologytoday.com/blog/the-compassion-chronicles/201307/how-compassion-can-heal-shame-childhood

[139] Germer, C. K., & Neff, K. D. (2013). Self-Compassion in Clinical Practice. *Journal of Clinical Psychology, 69*(8), 856-867. doi:10.1002/jclp.22021

[140] McGonigal, K. (2012). *The neuroscience of change: a compassion-based program for personal transformation*. Sounds True.

[141] Vettese, L. C., Dyer, C. E., Li, W. L., & Wekerle, C. (2011). Does Self-Compassion Mitigate the Association Between Childhood Maltreatment and Later Emotion Regulation Difficulties? A Preliminary Investigation. *International Journal of Mental Health and Addiction, 9*(5), 480-491.

[142] Engel, B. (2013, July 14). How Compassion Can Heal Shame from Childhood. Retrieved from https://www.psychologytoday.com/blog/the-compassion-chronicles/201307/how-compassion-can-heal-shame-childhood

[143] Benedict, F. (2014, September 12). The Courage of Self-Connection (Another Self-Compassion Tool). Retrieved February 05, 2017, from https://lifestarcentralvalley.wordpress.com/2014/08/13/the-courage-of-self-connection-another-self-compassion-tool/

[144] Ghali, E. (2015). Self- Compassion as a Mediator and Moderator of the Relationship between Psychological Suffering and Psychological Well-being among Palestinian Widowed Women. *Research on Humanities and Social Sciences, 5*(24), 66-76.

[145] Neff, K. (2015, February 21). The Physiology of Self-Compassion. Retrieved from http://self-compassion.org/the-physiology-of-self-compassion/

[146] McGonigal, K. (2012). *The neuroscience of change: a compassion-based program for personal transformation*. Sounds True.

[147] Flores, P. J. (2004). *Addiction as an attachment disorder*. Lanham: Jason Aronson.

[148] Neff, K. (2015, February 21). The Physiology of Self-Compassion. Retrieved from http://self-compassion.org/the-physiology-of-self-compassion/

[149] McGonigal, K. (2012). *The neuroscience of change: a compassion-based program for personal transformation*. Sounds True.

[150] Neff, K. (2015, February 21). The Physiology of Self-Compassion. Retrieved from http://self-compassion.org/the-physiology-of-self-compassion/

[151] Frye, T. (n.d.). Lecture presented at Counseling Sexual Addictions Class in Fresno Pacific Biblical Seminary, Fresno, CA.

[152] Neff, K. (2015, February 21). The Physiology of Self-Compassion. Retrieved from http://self-compassion.org/the-physiology-of-self-compassion/

[153] Vettese, L. C., Dyer, C. E., Li, W. L., & Wekerle, C. (2011). Does Self-Compassion Mitigate the Association Between Childhood Maltreatment and Later Emotion

Regulation Difficulties? A Preliminary Investigation. *International Journal of Mental Health and Addiction, 9*(5), 480-491.

[154] Neff, K. (2015, December 13). Exercise 2: Self-Compassion Break . Retrieved from http://self-compassion.org/exercise-2-self-compassion-break/

[155] McGonigal, K. (2012). *The neuroscience of change: a compassion-based program for personal transformation.* Sounds True.

[156] Benedict, F. (2014, August 16). Recovering from Relapse. Retrieved from https://lifestarcentralvalley.wordpress.com/2014/08/16/recovering-from-relapse

[157] McGonigal, K. (2012). *The neuroscience of change: a compassion-based program for personal transformation.* Sounds True.

[158] McGonigal, K. (2012). *The neuroscience of change: a compassion-based program for personal transformation.* Sounds True.

[159] McGonigal, K. (2012, February 01). The Willpower Instinct. Retrieved from https://www.youtube.com/watch?v=V5BXuZL1HAg&t=1s

[160] Eisler, M. (2017, January 11). A Meditation to Get Your Goals Back on Track. Retrieved from https://mindfulminutes.com/meditation-get-goals-back-track/

[161] Created by Forest Benedict, adapted from Dr. Kristin Neff's Self-compassion Break, Used with permission

[162] McGonigal, K. (2012, February 01). The Willpower Instinct. Retrieved from https://www.youtube.com/watch?v=V5BXuZL1HAg&t=1s

[163] Quote by Evander Holyfield

[164] Benedict, F. (2015, November 18). Pursuing Peace When the World's At War. Retrieved from https://lifestarcentralvalley.wordpress.com/2015/11/18/pursuing-peace-when-the-worlds-at-war

[165] University of Washington. (n.d.). Urge Surfing. Retrieved from http://depts.washington.edu/abrc/mbrp/recordings/Urge%20Surfing.mp3

[166] Henslin, E. R., & Johnson, B. F. (2008). *This is your brain on joy: a revolutionary program for balancing mood, restoring brain health, and nurturing spiritual growth.* Nashville, TN: Thomas Nelson.

[167] Neff, K. (2015, February 21). The Physiology of Self-Compassion. Retrieved from http://self-compassion.org/the-physiology-of-self-compassion/

[168] 1 John 4:18; Holy Bible, NIV

[169] From the song "Let There Be Peace on Earth" by Jill Jackson and Sy Miller. Copyright 1955, 1983 by Jan-Lee Music (ASCAP.) Used by Permission; all rights reserved.

[170] Benedict, F. (2014, September 19). The Time Travelers: Making Changes that Matter. Retrieved from https://lifestarcentralvalley.wordpress.com/2014/09/19/the-time-travelers-making-changes-that-matter/

[171] McGonigal, K. (2012, February 01). *The willpower instinct.* Retrieved from https://www.youtube.com/watch?v=V5BXuZL1HAg&t=1s

[172] McGonigal, K. (2012, February 01). *The willpower instinct.* Retrieved from https://www.youtube.com/watch?v=V5BXuZL1HAg&t=1s

[173] McGonigal, K. (2012, February 01). *The willpower instinct.* Retrieved from https://www.youtube.com/watch?v=V5BXuZL1HAg&t=1s

[174] McGonigal, K. (2012, February 01). *The willpower instinct.* Retrieved from https://www.youtube.com/watch?v=V5BXuZL1HAg&t=1s

[175] McGonigal, K. (2012, February 01). *The willpower instinct.* Retrieved from https://www.youtube.com/watch?v=V5BXuZL1HAg&t=1s. Exercise modified from McGonigal's recommendation.

[176] McGonigal, K. (2012, February 01). *The willpower instinct.* Retrieved from https://www.youtube.com/watch?v=V5BXuZL1HAg&t=1s. Exercise modified from McGonigal's recommendation.

[177] McGonigal, K. (2012, February 01). *The willpower instinct.* Retrieved from https://www.youtube.com/watch?v=V5BXuZL1HAg&t=1s

[178] Benedict, F. (2016, October 20). Connected Sex: A Paradigm Shift for the Sexually Addicted. Retrieved from https://lifestarcentralvalley.wordpress.com/2016/10/20/connected-sex-a-paradigm-shift-for-the-sexually-addicted

[179] Johnson, S. (2015, July 28). The New Frontier of Sex & Intimacy. Retrieved from https://www.youtube.com/watch?v=hiVijMLH2-k

[180] Johnson, S. (2017). Three Kinds of Sex. Retrieved from http://www.drsuejohnson.com/attachment-sex/three-kinds-sex/#more-185

[181] Johnson, S. (2017). Three Kinds of Sex. Retrieved from http://www.drsuejohnson.com/attachment-sex/three-kinds-sex/#more-185

[182] Zapf, J. L., Greiner, J., & Carroll, J. (2008). Attachment Styles and Male Sex Addiction. *Sexual Addiction & Compulsivity, 15*(2), 158-175.

[183] Hatch, L. (2012, February 15). Why is Sex Addiction Called an Intimacy Disorder? Retrieved from http://www.sexaddictionscounseling.com/why-is-sex-addiction-called-an-intimacy-disorder/

[184] Sexaholics Anonymous. (1989-2002). Sexaholics Anonymous. SA Literature. 40-41.

[185] Sexaholics Anonymous. (1989-2002). Sexaholics Anonymous. SA Literature. 42.

[186] Elements Behavioral Health. (2013, November 15). Sexual Anorexia Within Sexual Addiction. Retrieved from http://www.hypersexualdisorders.com/sex-addiction/sexual-anorexia-within-sexual-addiction/

[187] Katehakis, A. (2014, August 12). The Devastating Pain of 'Sexual Anorexics' Retrieved from https://www.psychologytodahttps://www.psychologytoday.com/blog/sex-lies-trauma/201408/the-devastating-pain-sexual-anorexics

[188] Katehakis, A. (2014, August 12). The Devastating Pain of 'Sexual Anorexics' Retrieved from https://www.psychologytodahttps://www.psychologytoday.com/blog/sex-lies-trauma/201408/the-devastating-pain-sexual-anorexics

[189] Bercaw, B., & Bercaw, G. (2010). *The Couple's Guide to Intimacy: How Sexual Reintegration Therapy Can Help Your Relationship Heal.* California Center for Healing. 7.

[190] Katehakis, A., & Schore, A. N. (2016). *Sex addiction as affect dysregulation: a neurobiologically informed holistic treatment.* New York: W.W. Norton & Company.

[191] Johnson, S. (2017). Three Kinds of Sex. Retrieved from http://www.drsuejohnson.com/attachment-sex/three-kinds-sex/#more-185

[192] Johnson, S. (2015, July 28). The New Frontier of Sex & Intimacy. Retrieved from https://www.youtube.com/watch?v=hiVijMLH2-k

[193] Reid, R. C., & Woolley, S. R. (2006). Using Emotionally Focused Therapy for Couples to Resolve Attachment Ruptures Created by Hypersexual Behavior. *Sexual Addiction & Compulsivity, 13*(2-3), 219-239.

[194] Weiss, R. (n.d.). Sex Addicts and "Sexual Sobriety". Retrieved February 13, 2017, from https://blogs.psychcentral.com/sex/2012/08/sexual-sobriety/

[195] Johnson, S. (2015, July 28). The New Frontier of Sex & Intimacy. Retrieved from https://www.youtube.com/watch?v=hiVijMLH2-k

[196] Bercaw, B., & Bercaw, G. (2010). *The Couple's Guide to Intimacy: How Sexual Reintegration Therapy Can Help Your Relationship Heal*. California Center for Healing. 11.

[197] Katehakis, A., & Schore, A. N. (2016). *Sex addiction as affect dysregulation: a neurobiologically informed holistic treatment*. New York: W.W. Norton & Company.

[198] Laaser, M. R. (2004). *Healing the wounds of sexual addiction*. Grand Rapids, MI: Zondervan. 182.

[199] Benedict, F. (2016, July 20). What's Your Recovery Anthem? Retrieved from https://lifestarcentralvalley.wordpress.com/2016/07/20/whats-your-recovery-anthem

[200] Webb, J. (n.d.). About Emotional Neglect. Retrieved from http://www.drjonicewebb.com/about-emotional-neglect/

[201] Hatch, L. (2012, February 15). Why is Sex Addiction Called an Intimacy Disorder? Retrieved from http://www.sexaddictionscounseling.com/why-is-sex-addiction-called-an-intimacy-disorder/

[202] Frye, T. (2010, September 27). *Intimacy disorder and sexual addiction*. Retrieved from https://www.youtube.com/watch?v=KeXfs2A84Hs&t=137s

[203] Benedict, F. (2015, November 26). Holiday Recipes for Relapse & Recovery (Revised). Retrieved from https://lifestarcentralvalley.wordpress.com/2014/11/20/holiday-recipes-for-relapse-recovery-revised

[204] LaPierre, J. (2013, March 09). Habits & Routines Make Recovery & Life Manageable. Retrieved February 06, 2017, from http://recoveryrocks.bangordailynews.com/2013/03/09/addiction/habits-routines-make-recovery-life-manageable/

[205] McGonigal, K. (2012). The willpower instinct: how self-control works, why it matters, and what you can do to get more of it. New York: Avery.

[206], McGonigal, K. (2012, February 01). The Willpower Instinct. Retrieved from https://www.youtube.com/watch?v=V5BXuZL1HAg&t=1s

[207] McGonigal, K. (2012). The willpower instinct: how self-control works, why it matters, and what you can do to get more of it. New York: Avery.

[208] University of Washington. (n.d.). Urge Surfing. Retrieved from http://depts.washington.edu/abrc/mbrp/recordings/Urge%20Surfing.mp3

[209] Benedict, F. (2016, July 04). The 4 Secrets of a Successful Summer Vacation (In Recovery). Retrieved from https://lifestarcentralvalley.wordpress.com/2016/07/04/the-4-secrets-of-a-successful-summer-vacation-in-recovery

[210] Benedict, F. (2014, December 25). A Connected Christmas: The Secret to Avoiding Auto-Pilot and Making Today Meaningful. Retrieved from https://lifestarcentralvalley.wordpress.com/2014/12/25/a-connected-christmas-the-secret-to-avoiding-auto-pilot-and-making-today-meaningful/

[211] Benedict, F. (2016, August 17). Out of Our Pain Comes Our Purpose. Retrieved from https://lifestarcentralvalley.wordpress.com/2016/08/16/out-of-our-pain-comes-our-purpose

[212] Benedict, F. (2016, May 24). *Vote for love*. Retrieved from https://lifestarcentralvalley.wordpress.com/2016/05/24/vote-for-love-by-forest-benedict-lmft-satp-c

Benedict, F. (2016, June 3). *Vote for love - not porn - fresno*. Retrieved from http://www.fresnobee.com/opinion/readers-opinion/article81475177.html

[213] Hilton, D. J. (2010, September 08). Donald L. Hilton Jr., MD speaks to Youth and Parents about Pornography and its impact on the Brain. Retrieved from https://www.youtube.com/watch?v=0ADYe5w75yk

[214] Deem, G. (2014, June 9). Porn: Many Teens Watch It, and Two Reasons That's a Problem. Retrieved from http://www.huffingtonpost.com/gabe-deem/porn-many-teens-watch-it-_b_5450478.html gtonpost.com/gabe-deem/porn-many-teens-watch-it-_b_5450478.html

[215] Pornography and Sex Trafficking. (n.d.). Trafficking Within the Professional Porn Industry. Retrieved from http://stoptraffickingdemand.com/trafficking-within-the-industry/

[216] Fight The New Drug. (2014, August 4). The Porn Industry's Dark Secrets. Retrieved from http://fightthenewdrug.org/the-porn-industrys-dark-secrets/

[217] Benedict, F. (2015, February 6). What One Person Can Do to Stand Against. Retrieved from https://lifestarcentralvalley.wordpress.com/2015/02/06/what-one-person-can-do-to-stand-against-shades-of-grey-by-forest-benedict-ma-satp-c-mft-intern-63601 and in The Fresno Bee:
Benedict, F. (2015, February 13). Forest Benedict: What one person can do to stand against "fifty shades of grey". Retrieved February 06, 2017, from http://www.fresnobee.com/opinion/readers-opinion/article19535103.html

[218] Bonomi, A. E., Altenburger, L. E., & Walton, N. L. (2013). "Double Crap!" Abuse and Harmed Identity in Fifty Shades of Grey. *Journal of Women's Health, 22*(9), 733-744

[219] American Family Association, Inc. (n.d.). A guide to what one person can do about pornography. Retrieved from www.macbma.net/uploads/6/5/7/9/657914/what_can_one_person_do.pdf

[220] "The only thing necessary for the triumph of evil is for good people to do nothing." Edmund Burke (n.d.).

[221] https://www.facebook.com/groups/TheAntiPornMovement/

[222] Manning, B. (2002). *Abba's child: the cry of the heart for intimate belonging*. Colorado Springs, CO: NavPress.

[223] Brown, B. (2012). *Daring greatly: how the courage to be vulnerable transforms the way we live, love, parent, and lead*. New York, NY: Gotham Books.

[224] Benedict, F. (2015, February 05). What One Person Can Do: The Ripple Effects of Living in Alignment. Retrieved from https://forestbenedict.com/2016/02/05/what-one-person-can-do-the-ripple-effects-of-living-in-alignment/
Benedict, F. (2015, February 16). What One Person Can Do: The Ripple Effects of Living in Alignment. Retrieved from https://lifestarcentralvalley.wordpress.com/2015/02/16/standing-together-against-shades-of-grey- the-birth-of-a-movement-by-forest-benedict-ma-satp-c-mft-intern-63601/

[225] Manning, B. (2002). *Abba's child: the cry of the heart for intimate belonging*. Colorado Springs, CO: NavPress.

[226] Manning, B. (2002). *Abba's child: the cry of the heart for intimate belonging*. Colorado Springs, CO: NavPress.

[227] Litster, T. (n.d.) - Beach Prophet podcast

228 Greer, R. J. (2012). *If you know who you are you will know what to do: living with integrity*. Nashville, TN: Abingdon. 80.

229 Attributed to Mahatma Gandhi

230 Benedict, F. (2015, June 18). "Dear Porn": A Father's Poignant Plan to Protect his Kids. Retrieved from http://protectyoungminds.org/2015/06/18/dear-porn-a-fathers-poignant-plan-to-protect-his-kids/

231 http://www.MensFraternity.com

232 Sprout, S., LCSW, CSAT. (2016, December 15). [E-mail].

233 Sprout, S., LCSW, CSAT. (2016, December 15). [E-mail].

234 McManus, E. (2016, December 01). For a Future Generation. Retrieved from https://www.youtube.com/watch?v=XylZOqozIXo

235 Pisor, R. (2016, December 17). [E-mail].

236 Pisor, R. (2016, December 17). [E-mail].

237 Sprout, S., LCSW, CSAT. (2016, December 15). [E-mail].

238 Pisor, R. (2016, December 17). [E-mail].

239 Pisor, R. (2016, December 17). [E-mail].

240 Litster, T. (n.d.) *Addiction*, Beach Prophet Podcast.

241 McManus, E. (2016, December 01). For a Future Generation. Retrieved from https://www.youtube.com/watch?v=XylZOqozIXo

242 McManus, E. (2008). *Wide Awake The Future Is Waiting Within You*. Gardners Books. 9.

243 Dyer, W. (2005, June). Seven Secrets Of A Joyful Life. Retrieved February 06, 2017, from http://www.drwaynedyer.com/press/seven-secrets-joyful-life/

244 Some questions based on the "Ask the Counselor" section on http://www.bethesdaworkshops.org/resources/counseling

245 Dallas, J. (2005). *The game plan*. Nashville, TN: W Pub. Group.

246 Benedict, F. (2014). *Healing Through Connection: A Blueprint for Long-Term Recovery* [Workbook].

247 Fradd, M. (2015, August 14). 8 Ways to Rebuild Trust with Your Wife. Retrieved from https://www.youtube.com/watch?v=JLa7Fu-ixdY

248 Benedict, F. (2014, September 06). Are We Having Fun Yet? Retrieved February 06, 2017, from https://lifestarcentralvalley.wordpress.com/2014/09/06/are-we-having-fun-yet/

249 Flores, P. J. (2004). *Addiction as an attachment disorder*. Lanham: Jason Aronson.

250 Paturel, A. (2014). Game Theory: How do video games affect the developing brains of children and teens? *Neurology Now, 10*(3), 32-36.

251 Weiss, R. (2013, September 25). "Thanks for Sharing" Nails It With Cross-Addictions. Retrieved from https://www.psychologytoday.com/blog/love-and-sex-in-the-digital-age/201309/thanks-sharing-nails-it-cross-addictions

252 Laaser (Source unknown)

253 Katehakis, A., & Schore, A. N. (2016). *Sex addiction as affect dysregulation: a neurobiologically informed holistic treatment*. New York: W.W. Norton & Company.

17316460R00157

Printed in Great Britain
by Amazon